Disasters' Impact on Drug Supply

Peggy J. Infante

Dedication

I dedicate this research and Praxis to my husband, family, and friends, all of whom encouraged and supported me on every step of this wild ride. To my mom and nana, who showed me what it means to be an intelligent, strong, independent woman and to chase the dream no matter the size. To my friends, who offered words of encouragement when I couldn't provide them to myself. To my husband, Michael, my biggest fan, and number one supporter. He reminded me every day that I am smart enough to reach this goal and can do anything I put my mind to. And to myself, for working hard and getting it done, even on the hardest of days.

Acknowledgments

I would like to thank my advisor, Dr. Daniyal Ali, for his guidance and support through this process as well as thank the committee members for their feedback.

Abstract of Praxis

In the United States, the rate of drug shortages has significantly increased over the last 10–15 years. The Food and Drug Administration passed the Food and Drug Administration Safety and Innovation Act in 2012, which requires pharmaceutical manufacturers to notify the administration of any changes to drug product production with the hope to prevent or mitigate any potential drug shortages. Various factors as to why drug shortages occur have been studied, including manufacturing difficulties, shortages of raw materials, voluntary recalls, natural disasters, supply and demand issues, business and economic issues, and regulatory issues.

This praxis focuses specifically on how global disasters affect raw material lead times and the associated delays, which lead to production disruptions and drug shortages. The data collected for this research praxis was gathered from the Food and Drug Administration's Drug Shortage Database, EM-DAT, a global database of disasters, and private industry information. The data was combined into a single dataset that represented the numerous variables that contribute to lead time delay.

Once compiled, CART Classification and Cluster Analysis were run on the data to determine the important variables that would serve as the final input variables. These input variables were then processed through Weka and various machine learning

algorithms to build a predictive model to forecast whether raw material lead time delay would occur. The results from the best performing predictive model showed that the model could predict lead time delay with an accuracy of 79.36% and a "yes delay" true positive rate of 0.511, indicating a "good" quality model.

These findings indicate that there is a relationship between global disasters and the occurrence of raw material lead time delay that can lead to potential drug shortages in the United States. Future research should be conducted to narrow down the output from a broad categorical response to a numerical response of a more exact timeframe.

Table of Contents

Dedication iv

Acknowledgments v

Abstract of Praxis vi

List of Figures xi

List of Symbols xv

List of Abbreviations and Acronyms xvii

Glossary of Terms xviii

Chapter 1–Introduction 1

1.1 Background 1

1.2 Research Motivation 2

1.3 Problem Statement 3

1.4 Thesis Statement 4

1.5 Research Objectives 4

1.6 Research Questions and Hypotheses 5

1.7 Scope of Research 6

1.8 Research Limitations 7

1.9 Organization of Praxis 7

Chapter 2–Literature Review 9

2.1 Introduction 9

2.2 Drug Shortages in the United States 9

2.3 Excipient and Active Ingredient Global Supply 12

2.4 Pharmaceutical Supply Chain Mitigation Strategies 17

2.5 Global Disasters and the Pharmaceutical Industry 20

2.6 Predictive Analytics 23

2.7 Previous Research on Drug Shortage Factors 25

2.8 Summary and Conclusion 27

Chapter 3–Methodology 28

3.1 Introduction 28

3.2 Independent Variable Selection 30

3.3 Data Collection and Dataset Construction 30

3.4 Variable Optimization and Dataset Simplification 34

3.5 Machine Learning Model Development and Testing 37

3.6 Data Preparation for Machine Learning Runs 47

3.7 Performance Metrics 51

3.8 Validation of Machine Learning Models 58

3.9 Comparison of Machine Learning Models 58

3.10 Chi-Squared Testing... 59

Chapter 4–Results 60

4.1 Introduction 60

4.2 Testing and Results–Research Question 1 and Hypothesis 1 60

4.3 Testing and Results–Research Question 2 and Hypothesis 2 65

4.4 Hypothesis 3 Testing and Results 87

4.5 Summary 92

Chapter 5–Discussion and Conclusions 94

5.1 Discussion 94

5.1.1 Discussion – Research Question 1 and Hypothesis 1 94

5.1.2 Discussion – Research Question 2 and Hypothesis 2 94

5.1.3 Discussion – Research Question 3 and Hypothesis 3 96

5.2 Conclusions 97

5.3 Contributions to Body of Knowledge 98

5.4 Recommendations for Future Research 100

List of Figures

Figure 2-1: New Shortages by Year, 2001 to 2023 11

Figure 2-2: Global Production of Active Pharmaceutical Ingredients 14

Figure 2-3. Supply Chain of Pharmaceutical Products..18

Figure 2-4: Types of Analytics for Pharmaceutical Manufacturing (Owczarek, 2021)...25

Figure 3-1: High Level Block Diagram……………………………………………….29

Figure 3-2: Visual Representation of Ensemble Learning………………………….....38

Figure 3-3: Visual Representation of Bagging/Bootstrap Aggregation Algorithm…......39

Figure 3-4: Visual Representation of Binary Decision Trees……………………….....40

Figure 3-5: Visual Representation of J48 Algorithm…………………………………..41

Figure 3-6: Visual Representation of REP Tree Algorithm…………………………....42

Figure 3-7: Visual Representation of Classification Algorithms………………….…..45

Figure 3-8: Visual Representation of JRip Algorithm……………………………….…46

Figure 3-9: Visual Representation of Filtered Classifier Algorithm……………….…..47

Figure 3-10: Visual Representation of Train/Test Split………………………………..49

Figure 3-11: Visual Representation of k-fold Cross Validation……………………....51

Figure 3-12: Confusion Matrix…………………………………………………………53

Figure 4-1: Cluster Analysis-Dendrogram ……………. ………...………………….. 62

Figure 4-2: CART Classification ……………………………………………………..64

Figure 4-3: Decision Tree Output from Weka for J48 Algorithm Runs ……..……….70

Figure 4-4: Decision Tree Output from Weka for REPTree Algorithm Runs………….73

Figure 4-5: List of Rules from Weka for JRip Algorithm Runs ………………………..78

Figure 4-6: Decision Tree Output from Weka for Filtered Classifier Algorithm Runs.80

Figure 4-7: Country Occurrences 2016-2022………………………………………..…...92

List of Tables

Table 3-1: Variables in Research Dataset………………………………………………34

Table 3-2: Sample Research Dataset……………………………………………………37

Table 4-1: Cluster Analysis Results……………………………………………………..61

Table 4-2: Bagging/Bootstrap Aggregation Algorithm – Default Parameters, 10-Fold Cross Validation……………………………………………………………………………68

Table 4-3: Bagging Algorithm – Default Parameters, 70/30 Train/Test Split…………...68

Table 4-4: J48 Algorithm – Default Parameters, 10-Fold Cross Validation……………69

Table 4-5: J48 Algorithm – Default Parameters, 70/30 Train/Test Split………………..71

Table 4-6: REP Tree Algorithm – Default Parameters, 10-Fold Cross Validation……..72

Table 4-7: REP Tree Algorithm – Default Parameters, 70/30 Train/Test Split…………73

Table 4-8: Voted Perceptron Algorithm – Default Parameters, 10-Fold Cross Validation…………………………………………………………………………………...74

Table 4-9: Voted Perceptron Algorithm – Default Parameters, 70/30 Train/Test Split...75

Table 4-10: JRip Algorithm – Default Parameters, 10-Fold Cross Validation…………..76

Table 4-11: JRip Algorithm – Default Parameters, 70/30 Train/Test Split……………...77

Table 4-12: Filtered Classifier Algorithm – Default Parameters, 10-Fold Cross Validation……………………………………………………………………………...…79

Table 4-13: Filtered Classifier Algorithm – Default Parameters, 70/30 Train/Test Split.80

Table 4-14: Machine Learning Model Results Comparison Part I……………………...82

Table 4-15: Machine Learning Model Results Comparison Part II…………………….83

Table 4-16: Machine Learning Model Results Weight Average Comparison…………..84

Table 4-17: Comprehensive Comparison of Machine Learning Models..................88

Table 4-18: Chi-Square Test for Country and Yes/No Delay..............................91

List of Symbols

X–Input

Y–Output

ML–Machine Learning

e–Euler's number (2.718…)

P–probability

μ–mean (average)

m–independent and identically distributed variables, sample size

E(X)–expected value

ε–based on already known values

θ–set of parameters

Exp–exponent

H–classifier

$h_{a,c}$–defined classifier

R–desired value

a–value in set

∈–in the set

E–parameter setting

N–parameter setting

Sign–signum function

w–vector of real-valued weights

b–bias

$\hat{Y}$–expected value for y

TP–True Positive

TN–True Negative

FP–False Positive

FN–False Negative

P–Positive

N–Negative

PPV–Positive Predicted Value

TC–True Correctly Classified

FC–Falsely Classified

K–Cohen's Kappa

List of Abbreviations and Acronyms

FDA–Food and Drug Administration

FDASIA–Food and Drug Administration Safety and Innovation Act

API–Active Pharmaceutical Ingredient

COVID-19–Coronavirus Disease 2019

EM-DAT–Emergency Event Database

ASHP–American Society of Health-System Pharmacists

USP–United States Pharmacopeia

DMF–Drug Master File

NIH–National Institute of Health

SML–Small, Medium, Large

MCC–Matthews Correlation Coefficient

AUC–Area Under the Curve

ROC–Receiver Operating Characteristics

PRC–Precision Recall Curve

Glossary of Terms

agglomerative clustering–hierarchical grouping of objects into clusters of similarity.

bifolious–clades having two leaves.

binders–improve bonding ability of pharmaceutical products.

coatings/films–substances that surround a product.

coloring agents–substance that provides color.

dendrogram–tree diagram showing relationships.

diluents–filler material in pharmaceutical products.

disintegrants–improve the dissolving ability of pharmaceutical products.

excipient–inactive substance.

glidants/lubricants–improve powder flow in pharmaceutical products.

hyperplane–decision boundary splitting inputs into regions.

overfitting–model that can model training data but not new data.

simplicifolious–clades having one leaf.

underfitting: model that can't model the training data or new data.

Chapter 1–Introduction

1.1 Background

Medical drug products are regulated under the U. S. Food and Drug Administration (FDA), a federal government agency. One of the main objectives of the FDA is to protect the public by ensuring the safety and efficacy of drugs, biological products, and medical devices (FDA, 2018). Another responsibility of the FDA is to alert the public of drug product recalls and shortages. A drug shortage as defined by the FDA is "a situation in which the total supply of all clinically interchangeable versions of an FDA-regulated drug is inadequate to meet the current or projected demand at the patient level" (U.S. Food and Drug Administration, 2012, p. 8). The passage of the Food and Drug Administration Safety and Innovation Act (FDASIA) in 2012 required manufacturers to notify the FDA of any changes to the production of finished drug products with the hope that the agency can then help to reduce the possibility of further shortages or find strategies to prevent the shortage from happening altogether. A yearly summary report of drug shortage and the FDA's strategies to mitigate or prevent that shortage is compiled and presented to Congress as required by the Food and Drug Administration Safety and Innovation Act. Some of the reasons drug shortages occur are quality issues during manufacturing, production delays, and raw material procurement setbacks.

Pharmaceutical companies rely heavily on acquiring raw materials from global manufacturers and suppliers. However, with the frequency of natural and biological disasters around the globe, raw material, and active pharmaceutical ingredient (API) procurement has been increasingly challenging and has worsened the drug shortage problem in the United States. The scope of this research study is to present a solution to the global pharmaceutical material supply chain management problems faced by pharmaceutical companies. The research presented proposes a model that predicts possible delays in the lead times for active pharmaceutical ingredients and the excipients used in the final formulations of medicinal products based on global disasters, their locations, and historical lead times.

1.2 Research Motivation

Patient care is significantly impacted when a drug shortage exists and puts increased pressure on health care workers. When that happens, patients are more likely to be prescribed alternative medications, which hopefully provide the same or similar therapeutic benefits as the preferred drug. However, these alternatives may have dangerous side effects not commonly associated with the drug of choice that can in turn lead to more complications and the beginning of a never-ending and often desperate cycle. Being able to accurately predict the lead time delay for pharmaceutical raw materials and active pharmaceutical ingredients would assist global pharmaceutical manufacturers in optimizing production schedules to prevent further drug shortages and relieve pressure on patients, hospitals, and health care workers.

From the perspective of the individuals working in pharmaceutical manufacturing plants, being able to accurately schedule commercial batches that go to market and clinical batches that are headed for trials is crucial. As seen during the peak of the COVID-19 pandemic, lead times for raw materials were quite unpredictable, which caused manufacturing schedules to be delayed and unpredictable. Proper supply chain management is important for pharmaceutical companies to run efficiently. Therefore, having a clear understanding of what raw material lead times look like and if a delay may occur based on global natural and biological disasters can help streamline manufacturing operations and assist in decreasing the likelihood of future drug shortages.

1.3 Problem Statement

Pandemics, disruptions, and disasters related to inefficiencies in global pharmaceutical supply chain management strategies have led to drug shortages and production scheduling delays.

Pharmaceutical supply chain management strategies have traditionally taken into consideration financial crises but have failed to develop an understanding of how global disruptions can cause availability issues for manufacturing and production. This was especially apparent during the COVID-19 pandemic, when international shipments were delayed or cancelled that in turn caused a lack of inventory at the pharmaceutical manufacturing sites. These inefficient systems that cause production scheduling delays contribute to furthering the potential for drug shortages in the United States.

1.4 Thesis Statement

A predictive model for forecasting raw material lead time delay is required to help U.S. pharmaceutical companies prevent production scheduling delays leading to further drug shortages.

In an analysis done by the FDA in 2019, it was noted that 72% of active pharmaceutical ingredient manufacturers that supply to the United States market were located overseas (Raghavendran & Christian, 2022), which appears to also be the case with raw material suppliers. With the unpredictability of global natural and biological disasters, the expected lead times of excipients and APIs has caused manufacturing instability that have led to drug shortages in the United States. By statistically analyzing historical data, predicting future behaviors of global suppliers can be better understood, which can help ease any production uncertainty experiences for pharmaceutical companies.

1.5 Research Objectives

The main objective of this research is to determine the prediction accuracy of raw material and active pharmaceutical ingredient lead times and thus identify possible delays based on global pandemics, disruptions, and disasters using a predictive model and statistical analysis techniques. The research objectives are the following:

1. Identify the optimal parameters related to raw material and active pharmaceutical ingredients seen in drug shortage products from 2016–2022, including

such issues as purchasing, cost, manufacturer location by state and country, and global pandemic, disruption, and disaster occurrence.

2. Design and develop a predictive model that uses statistical analysis techniques to identify lead times and delay occurrences of active and inactive drug ingredients from 2016–2022.

3. Evaluate and validate the predictive capability of the predictive model to predict the lead times and delay occurrence for the active and inactive ingredients of drug shortage products.

1.6 Research Questions and Hypotheses

The goal of this research is to develop an innovative tool that assists in predicting the lead times and delay occurrences of raw materials and active pharmaceutical ingredients based on the relationship between historical lead times measured in days, global disaster occurrence, and supplier location by state and country.

RQ1: What are the features that impact pharmaceutical raw material lead time delay?

RQ2: Can a predictive model be built to forecast raw material lead time delay?

RQ3: Were all countries impacted similarly due to disruptions in supplying pharmaceutical raw materials due to pandemics, disruptions, and disasters between 2016-2022?

H1: Features that impact pharmaceutical raw material lead time delay are historical lead time, raw material type, supplier location, and presence of pandemic/disruption/disaster.

H2: A predictive model that forecasts raw material lead time delay can decrease the chance of production disruptions that lead to drug shortages.

H3: Countries that supply the pharmaceutical industry's materials do not show similar disruption rates due to pandemics, disruptions, and disasters.

1.7 Scope of Research

The scope of this research is limited to the drug shortage products (their active pharmaceutical material and raw materials) from the years 2016 to 2022 in the United States as determined by the FDA. A total of 1,013 drug shortage products and 5,378 raw materials and active pharmaceutical ingredients of each drug shortage product was identified from the pharmaceutical companies' information packet that is included in the drug product's packaging. The global natural and biological disaster data is limited to January 1, 2016, to October 5, 2022. This information was retrieved from EM-DAT (Emergency Event Database), an international disasters database that is maintained by the Center for Research on the Epidemiology of Disasters (2023) at the School of Public Health at the Catholic University of Louvain in Brussels, Belgium.

1.8 Research Limitations

This research is limited to the approved medicinal drug products that were or are in shortage in the United States. The model has not been validated to reflect any industry besides pharmaceuticals and does not include any drug products that were approved in countries outside the United States. The data obtained focuses solely on the years 2016–2022, which specifically encompasses the global crisis of the COVID-19 pandemic. The values for the data were not statistically manipulated to balance any skewing. All the costs for active pharmaceutical ingredients and raw materials are in dollars per kilogram to allow consistency across the data. Any active pharmaceutical ingredients with limited or no data were excluded to keep all the data reliable and accurate. The types of global pandemics, disruptions, and disasters were limited to natural and biological events, as those are most likely to cause issues with shipping and receiving lead times and to determine the occurrence of delays.

1.9 Organization of Praxis

This praxis consists of five chapters that in total constitute an in-depth analysis of the impact of international pandemics, disasters, and disruptions on global pharmaceutical supply chain management. Chapter 1 introduces the research topic and presents the background information needed to begin the explanation of the research topic. Here the motivation for the research is detailed, along with the research questions and hypotheses. In addition, the problem statement, thesis statement, objectives, and limitations are discussed. The second chapter presents a literature review of relevant published research and research studies that have been conducted on the topic. Chapter 3 focuses on the methodology used in the research. A broad overview is presented, followed by explanations on how the data was collected, how the model was built, and how the data analysis methodologies were used. The fourth chapter summarizes the results obtained during data analysis. Finally, chapter 5 discusses the results and final conclusions of the study, as well as the main learnings and limitations during the study, and describes how the study analysis and results can contribute to future work.

Chapter 2–Literature Review

2.1 Introduction

Lead times for raw materials and active pharmaceutical ingredients and potential delays are of great concern for pharmaceutical companies globally. This concern has become particularly relevant because of the COVID-19 global pandemic. An increased awareness of how pandemics, global disasters, and other types of disruptions can affect lead times and create drug shortages has led pharmaceutical companies and manufacturers to adopt better supply chain management strategies to reduce future delays and prevent drug shortages.

This chapter presents a comprehensive review of pertinent literature regarding the topics addressed in this research study. The focus of the review is on (a) drug shortages in the United States, (b) raw material and active ingredient global supply information, (c) current pharmaceutical supply chain strategies, (d) global disasters and their effect on the pharmaceutical industry, and (e) predictive analytics in the pharmaceutical sector. The goal of the literature review is to provide a summary of the existing technical knowledge and research that has been conducted and published on the topic.

2.2 Drug Shortages in the United States

The FDA tracks shortages at the national level based on information from manufacturers about their ability to supply market demand. A drug is in shortage when the total supply of all versions of a commercially available product cannot meet the current demand.

The FDA works closely with pharmaceutical companies to prevent drug shortages from occurring that could impact patients. Risks to the drug supply come from unforeseen and unexpected occurrences, and in the face of such events, the FDA implements strategies that help companies to resolve the issues surrounding the shortages. According to the FDA (2022, para. 3), it can

- Expedite reviews of new production lines or material sources to increase production quickly,
- Extend product expiration dates, if it is safe to do that,
- Import medicines to the U.S. if they meet our safety and effectiveness criteria.

Even with the established existence of these strategies, pharmaceutical companies are required to inform the FDA of potential or existing manufacturing delays or drug product discontinuances and to provide a risk management plan that provides an option to reintroduce the product to the market.

The American Society of Health-System Pharmacists (ASHP) compiled national drug shortage data by year from January 2001 to the end of March 2023 as presented in Figure 2-1, which shows that the highest number of new drug shortages identified in a year occurred in 2011 at 267, followed by 185 in 2014, 186 in 2018, and 160 in 2022.

Figure 2-1: New Shortages by Year, 2001 to 2023

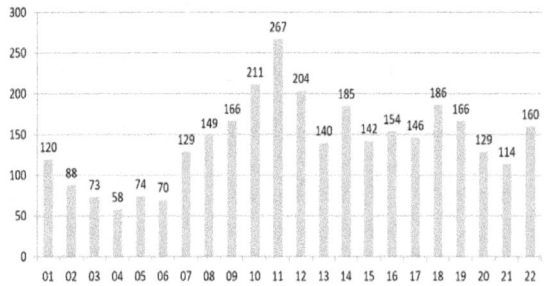

Source: ASHP. (2022). Drug shortages statistics. https://www.ashp.org/drug-shortages/shortage-resources/drug-shortages-statistics?loginreturnUrl=SSOCheckOnly (Permission to use image was obtained from the author.)

Despite a dramatic decline in 2023, ASHP concludes that shortages "are not resolving and new shortages are increasing," that "shortages are the highest since 2014," and that shortages "of local anesthetics and basic hospital drugs, albuterol solution, common oral and ophthalmic products, and ADHD treatments are affecting large numbers of organizations and patients" (ASHP, 2022, paras. 2–3).

Continuous drug shortages threaten public health by limiting access to life-saving drugs. The literature notes that operational transparency is required to mitigate drug shortages as explained in a 2012 mandate from the FDA. Pharmaceutical companies must report any challenges that could lead to a shortage. The goal of such mandates is to minimize the extent of a possible drug shortage by facing the problem directly. Open communication and transparency between government and pharmaceutical companies can help to alleviate strain on the supply chain, thus decreasing the potential for drug shortages (Lee et al., 2021).

Drug shortages can occur at any phase in the life cycle of a drug. However, the research showed the top causes were shortage of raw materials, manufacturer related issues, regulatory and legislative factors, and labor disruption. Shaya et al. also showed that 27% of drug shortages are caused by unexplained events. The group suggests that to implement successful programs to manage drug shortages, it is important to understand what causes a shortage, clear communication strategies, and involvement from all stakeholders in a health care system (Gu et al., 2011).

As Fox et al. (2014) has noted, the United States operates under a "just-in-time inventory distribution system" (p. 361), which means there is adequate supply available but not an excessive amount kept in stock. Fox et al. also explain that this type of distribution system is complex and can further delay drug products from reaching patients and forcing the health care providers to ration and make difficult decisions in terms of who gets treatment.

2.3 Excipient and Active Ingredient Global Supply

Pharmaceutical excipients in most cases are inert substances as described in an article by Haywood and Glass (2011). They explain that excipients are the inert substances that serve as delivery systems for medications, which allows various dosages to exist and function therapeutically. Most dosage forms are comprised of 90% excipients. The most common excipients are diluents, binders, disintegrants, glidants, lubricants, coatings, films, and coloring agents, all of which provide a certain function to the final medicinal dosage. Should they be interested, patients are able to learn and understand what excipients are in their medications by reading the consumer medicine information leaflet provided by the pharmaceutical manufacturer.

Excipients are the raw materials that are added to a drug for purposes other than the therapeutic or diagnostic effect of the drug (Dureja & Kumar, 2013) and play a key role in pharmaceutical products to enhance solubility and bioavailability of the medicinal active ingredient. In most countries, excipients are regulated in similar ways to their active ingredient counterparts, but the regulations do differ from country to country. To harmonize international regulations, the International Pharmaceutical Excipients Council was founded in 1991. Their responsibility is to regulate safety measures, introduce new products, and determine what industry standards are needed internationally.

The U.S. Food and Drug Administration gathered data on the reliance of the United States on foreign active pharmaceutical ingredient manufacturing based on location. The analysis showed that 72% of API manufacturing facilities that supply to the U.S. market is overseas (Raghavendran & Christian, 2022). This is an important concern for the stability of the U.S. medicinal supply chain because this reliance on foreign manufacturers can cause problems if a global disaster were to occur. The United States government responded to this issue by putting forth approximately $34 billion to improve the medicinal supply chain resilience. Figure 2-2 shows the global production of active pharmaceutical ingredients by value and by volume. The first chart shows that, by value, the U.S. produces the most APIs, followed by other countries, China, and India. The second chart shows that China produces the largest volume of APIs, followed by

Figure 2-2: Global Production of Active Pharmaceutical Ingredients

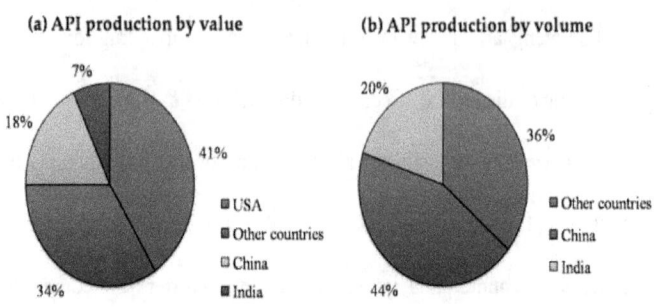

Source: Cherian et al. (2021). India's road to independence in manufacturing active pharmaceutical ingredients: Focus on essential medicines. *Economies, 9.* https://doi.org/10.3390/economies9020071. (Permission to use image obtained from the author.)

other countries and India. From this data, it is apparent that China and India supply the globe with most of the active pharmaceutical ingredients used in medicines.

The United States Pharmacopeia (USP) is an annual publication of the United States Pharmacopeial Convention that sets the standard for the identity, strength, quality, purity, packaging, and labeling for drug substances, dosage forms, and other therapeutic products. The USP gathers information from global manufacturers and suppliers in order to provide updated regulations for both excipients and active pharmaceutical ingredients. As part of the information regarding the active pharmaceutical ingredients, manufactures' drug master files (DMF), which provide "details about facilities, processes, components, or articles used in the manufacturing, processing, packaging, and storing of one or more APIs and/or human drugs" (Yehaskel, 2018, p. 1), was analyzed and the manufacturing location was determined. From that data, USP determined that India accounts for 48% of global DMFs, followed by Europe at 22%, China at 13%, and the U.S. at 10%.

Over the course of 20 years, India has increased its global production of active pharmaceutical ingredients from 20% in 2000 to 62% in 2021. China has also shown a 5% increase from 2019 to 2021. In contrast, Europe and the U.S. have both decreased the number of active ingredients produced from 2000 to 2021. With this knowledge, pharmaceutical companies can monitor where they source their active pharmaceutical ingredients and excipients, as well as determining the final dosage form.

Procurement of these materials plays a large and key role in understanding the global impact of the top producers of raw materials and APIs. Anand et al. (2016) defines procurement lead time as "the time required to acquire the supplies and services and then placing them in the hands of user." They explain that the process is complex and involves agencies, manufactures, and consumers. Lead time can be understood in two stages: internal and external. Internal lead time includes the steps that the consumer takes to place the order; external lead time is the time from when the order is placed until it is received. For the pharmaceutical industry, lead times can be used with excipients, active pharmaceutical ingredients, final dosage forms, packaging supplies, and any other product that is involved in the in practice of medicine.

As noted by Anand et al. (2016), effective procurement and manageable lead times can be highly impactful on inventory management and the ability to have, keep, and maintain a stock of items. Longer lead times can force manufacturing companies to delay production, which ultimately leads to a delay in a patient getting their medication.

The goal is to streamline the procurement process and optimize the lead time of raw materials and APIs to maintain schedules that prevent further delays while at the same time monitoring cost.

In an article written for *LinkedIn*, Wurm (2022) explains that lead times are one of the bottlenecks that pose a challenge to pharmaceutical manufacturers. The global supply chain for excipients and APIs has faced increasing challenges over the last two decades that caused manufacturing delays that led to drug shortages in the United States. With the nature of the pharmaceutical industry and the increase in research and development, the performance of excipient and API suppliers and manufacturers is of the utmost importance. When the demand for these products increases, the suppliers must manage the expectations of their customers, and, at the same time, pharmaceutical companies need to think strategically in how they plan their operations. Realistic timelines, safety stock quantities, and having access to alternative vendors would allow for pharmaceutical companies to plan appropriately and think creatively if issues were to arise with the suppliers (Wurm, 2022).

Lead times are one of the most challenging parts of supply chain management and have a huge impact on manufacturing. Developing optimal inventory systems to streamline a company's lead times is imperative. A study conducted by Adusumalli et al. (2019) at the Zaragoza Logistics Center in Zaragoza, Spain, analyzed that pharmaceutical company's inventory systems to help develop a model that would optimize inventory levels and lead times at the company. The goal of the study was to show a correlation between inventory and lead time. The company had an inventory of 53% of drug substances, which is understandable as that is what is the medicine in its final dosage becomes. However, to keep up with this quantity, an understanding of vendor and supplier lead times is required. With that information secured, it is possible to optimize the inventory/lead time relationship and potentially lower the lead time. This concept can be applicable to most industries but especially to pharmaceutical companies that work directly with material lead times and inventory sufficiency. Having a streamlined process and better understanding of the entire system can benefit companies as a whole and prevent drug shortages from occurring.

2.4 Pharmaceutical Supply Chain Mitigation Strategies

The pharmaceutical supply chain is a complex system in which medications are manufactured and supplied to patients and involves a multitude of stakeholders, including manufacturers, distributors, and pharmacy managers. Figure 2-3 shows an example of a typical pharmaceutical supply chain. The system faces challenges that determine whether or not a patient receives their proper medication in a timely manner. Of specific note is supply chain visibility, which for the pharmaceutical industry includes raw materials and active pharmaceutical ingredients.

Figure 2-3. Supply Chain of Pharmaceutical Products

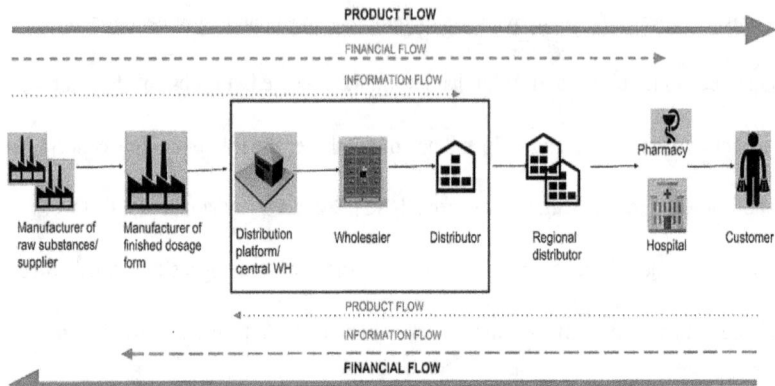

Note: Reprinted from (Rathipriya et al. (2022), Demand forecasting model for time-series pharmaceutical data using shallow and deep neural network model. *Neural Computing and Applications, 35*. https://doi.org/10.1007/s00521-022-07889-9 (Permission to use image obtained from the author.)

As noted by Kaylor (2020, para. 7), there are five basic steps to the pharmaceutical supply chain:

1. Drugs are manufactured at production sites.
2. They are then transferred to wholesale distributors.
3. The pharmaceuticals are stocked at various types of pharmacies, including retail and mail-order.
4. Pharmacy benefit management companies negotiate prices and process drugs through quality and utilization management checks.
5. Finally, pharmacies dispense the drugs to patients, who take them as prescribed.

For the whole network to function successfully to allow patients to get the medications they require, all parts must work in conjunction for everything to flow smoothly.

In general, the pharmaceutical supply chain is effective; however, it does face challenges that can impact the entire pipeline. The largest and most uncertain challenge occurs at the first step, where the pharmaceutical manufacturer must take into account the possibility of facing raw material and active pharmaceutical supply shortages. Inventory management offers a strategy to minimize the long-term effects of supply shortages that could lead to various types of manufacturing delay. Inventory management and supply chain monitoring are a mitigation strategy used by pharmaceutical companies to lower the chance of production delays from occurring that could lead to drug shortages.

The most difficult area of the whole pharmaceutical supply chain system therefore occurs at the manufacturing stage, which consists of (a) production of the active ingredient or excipient and (b) production of the final dosage form. Both have variable time frames due to reliance on receiving material. If materials are delayed in transit neither production can occur, thus making this the most complex and unpredictable stage of the supply chain process (Shah, 2004).

In a study regarding the reliability of the pharmaceutical supply chain and its effect on drug shortages, Tucker and Daskin (2022) explained that for there to be improvements, vulnerability and reliability in the supply chain needs to take into account, a crucial part of which is the lead time in the materials used in production. The authors note that 62% of drug shortages come from quality issues that arise in the manufacturing process. The rate of disruptions can be calculated to determine the potential rate of recovery from a drug shortage. The data gathered from the model showed that lean supply chains and quicker rates of recovery decrease the drug shortage potential by 5% or more.

2.5 Global Disasters and the Pharmaceutical Industry

During the COVID-19 pandemic, medication purchases increased dramatically, forcing demand to levels never seen in the United States. At the same time, pharmaceutical manufacturing plants were shutting down to slow the spread of the virus, which put massive pressure on the drug supply chain. As clinical pharmacist Christina M. Bookwalter (2021) noted, "pharmacists need to understand what is causing the drug shortages and how to ensure patient safety during the shortage (para. 1)". However, the added pressure of finding alternative drug treatments led to increasing the demand for those alternatives causing a shortage in those products, thus escalating the entire crisis.

When a crisis like the COVID-19 pandemic occurs, access to drug products quickly becomes an international concern. Burry et al. (2020) assessed mitigation strategies of drug supply at the local, institutional, and global levels during various crises and observed that stockpiling and hoarding of high-risk drug products occur at a higher level in higher income countries, which leaves middle to lower income countries struggling to find the supplies to meet ever increasing demands. This ultimately leads to drug shortages in the areas where access is already limited. The authors describe open and honest communication from large health organizations to be the biggest asset in preventing further shortages.

As noted by Bookwalter (2021), China is a major source of active pharmaceutical ingredients, finished drug products, and raw materials. During the pandemic, 37 Chinese pharmaceutical manufacturing plants were shutdown, forcing pharmaceutical companies to reevaluate their current stock and find alternate suppliers. Along the same lines, India is the largest global producer of generic drug products for themselves domestically and for U.S. companies. Seventy percent of the raw materials used in manufacturing at these pharmaceutical plants in India are imported from China. In response to the delays from China, which of course led to shortages in India, the Indian government mandated that all medication exports be suspended to prevent shortages in their own country, which forced shortages in other countries, which quickly spiraled out of control, resulting in a global drug shortage crisis.

To slow the spread of COVID-19, multiple countries across the globe restricted commercial and international trading channels, which only exasperated the global drug shortage crisis. Badreldin and Atallah (2020) explained that these measures that led to these shortages would have extended and negative impact on health care providers. The authors continued by noting the extensive research required for the medical industry to safely recommend alternate forms of treatment. In the process, patients were the most affected group and needed to be educated in alternative therapies to achieve the required relief.

The COVID-19 pandemic is of great current interest in understanding widespread drug shortages; however, other global disasters and disruptions have previously led to drug shortages as well. Hurricanes, floods, earthquakes, and other natural disasters have caused significant damage to numerous manufacturing plants, wreaking havoc on the pharmaceutical sector.

In 2017, Hurricane Maria devastated the island of Puerto Rico, claiming thousands of lives and causing numerous factories to close their doors for an undetermined amount of time. Kulaga (2018) notes that Puerto Rico is the main producer for over 100 pharmaceutical products, including drugs for heart disease, cancer, diabetes, arthritis, and HIV, along with IV bags. Notably, 43% of the IV solution market in the United States is produced in Puerto Rico. Facing the inability to make up for that loss of product, the U.S. healthcare system experienced an inability to properly treat patients needing IV solution bags. Although it is impossible to predict when a natural disaster will occur, having the proper preparations in place is important to mitigate drug shortages in a crisis (Tucker & Daskin, 2022).

Just as drug shortages occur in the United States, natural and biological disasters affect the drug supplies of other countries as well. Mori et al. (2012) identified the primary cause of the drug shortages that occurred after the 2022 earthquake in Japan to be the devastation of 24 pharmaceutical manufacturing plants and a single packaging plant. This type of destruction from a natural disaster is unpredictable and can affect any country, from under-developed to the most developed. The authors showed that drug shortage recovery did occur after 6 months of restoration, which is applicable to other countries as well. Disasters can occur at any time and pharmaceutical companies and their governments need to be prepared to handle the aftermath accordingly.

2.6 Predictive Analytics

Predictive analytics is a machine learning process that uses historical data to make predictions about future outcomes (Owczarek, 2021). Recent years have seen a significant increase in the use of predictive analytics in the pharmaceutical sector, especially in the manufacturing stage. Pharmaceutical companies can use predictive analysis to optimize inventory management, focus research and development, and distribute finished products. With a focus on supply chain, predictive analytics can help companies understand how demand could be affected by various global developments. Having a better understanding of possible changes can help to better prioritize available resources and future requested resources.

Using predictive analytics in understanding pharmaceutical data can be incredibly beneficial, the biggest benefit of which is the ability to make accurate decisions about manufacturing and future planning. Data analysis is useful in seeing patterns in marketing, operations, and cost reduction. Only the knowledge gained from predictive analytics can allow pharmaceutical companies to move towards growth and optimization. However, certain challenges come with this kind of analytics. In some situations, gathering data could be difficult if older manufacturing technology is being used. In the same way, having employees who are properly trained and understand data analysis can be a limitation in becoming a modern, optimized organization (Owczarek, 2021).

Predictive analytics can help pharmaceutical companies over time. Most companies function in a reactive mode, responding to what is currently going on in the moment rather than anticipating what might happen in the future. Being able to predict problems before they occur and having potential solutions to the problems at hand can improve manufacturing capabilities and allow for optimized processing. Owczarek (2021) sees the future of pharmaceutical manufacturing in terms of four distinctly different kinds of analytics: descriptive analytics, diagnostic analytics, predictive analytics, and prescriptive analytics (Figure 4). Each category has its own questions and reasoning for being beneficial. Descriptive analytics focuses on what happened and looks at information from the past. Diagnostic analytics questions why something occurred to gain insight on a specific event. Predictive analytics focuses on what could happen in the future based on what and why something occurred in the past. And lastly, prescriptive analytics looks at what can be done to prevent future similar occurrences from happening.

This type of analysis can be related to all areas of the pharmaceutical industry; however, manufacturing has been the focus of most of the relevant research. Nerveless the same analytics can be applied to research and development, marketing, distribution, and other areas to help optimize their processes and predict future outcomes.

In a study conducted by Liu et al, a predictive model was built to predict and manage drug shortages based on internal purchasing, formulary, and drug shortage data from 2016 to 2017. A multiple logistic regression model was chosen as the preferred algorithm for the desired output the dataset constructed by the authors. The model developed showed an accuracy of 0.87 (87%) using the 70/30 train/test split. (Liu et al.) This previous predictive analytics work allowed for an understanding of what potential accuracy could be for this research praxis.

Figure 2-4: Types of Analytics for Pharmaceutical Manufacturing (Owczarek, 2021)

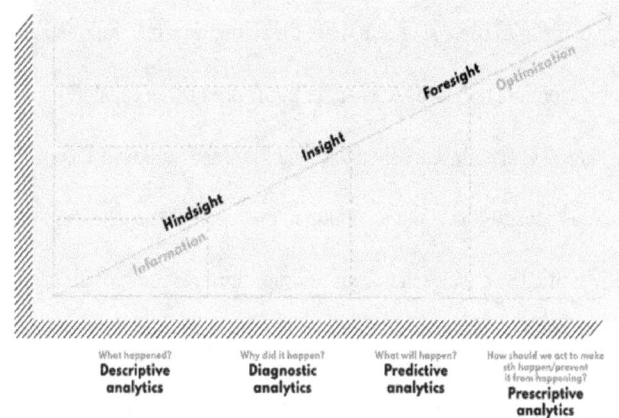

Source: Owczarek, D. (2021). Predictive analytics: A revolutionary tool for pharmaceutical manufacturing. Nexocode. https://nexocode.com/blog/posts/predictive-analytics-in-pharmaceutical-manufacturing (Permission to use image obtained from the author.)

2.7 Previous Research on Drug Shortage Factors

Various factors have been determined to lead to drug shortages that relate directly to the input variable options for the predictive model that will be built for this research praxis. Ventola mentions the following factors: manufacturing difficulties, shortages of raw materials, voluntary recalls, natural disasters, supply and demand issues, business and economic concerns, and regulatory issues. Manufacturing difficulties like older equipment, resource allocation and limited production capabilities are identified as a significant factor that can contribute to drug shortages because of the strict rules that must be followed as per the FDA. Many pieces of equipment and production lines are designated for certain products and are filed and approved with the FDA, if anything were to happen to either, it can lead to a potential shift in production causing a drug shortage to occur. Raw material shortages are a top factor that led to drug shortages because many companies use a single supplier for certain raw materials and any delay in production or discontinuation leads to changes in the production capabilities. Similarly, to manufacturing, raw materials are filed with the FDA and approved accordingly therefore a simple substitution is not an option to overcome this challenge. Natural disasters are identified as a factor that leads to drug shortages due to their effect on manufacturing facilities, shipping and receiving of raw materials, active ingredients, or finished products, and the effect that's possible on single product production companies that can lack capabilities to produce their product. Supply and demand issues are another factor identified to lead to drug shortages because on occasion, products are approved for new indications and the market changes where that product's demand is high, and the supply may not be at the same level.

Of these, natural disasters, shortages of raw materials, and supply and demand issues will be focused on more than the others. Natural disasters globally can lead to shifts in supply and demand and negatively impact manufacturing capabilities. Raw material shortages have a significant impact on the U.S. pharmaceutical industry because its dependence on materials imported from other countries. Supply and demand of raw materials and active pharmaceutical ingredients can put pressure on manufacturing that can easily lead to drug shortages. These previously studied factors will be investigated further as options for input variables for the research dataset that will be used in building the predictive model using Weka, a set of machine learning algorithms that help facilitate data mining (Ventola, 2011).

2.8 Summary and Conclusion

This literature review presented a thorough examination of academic papers, federal agency presentations, non-profit publications, and web articles on the pharmaceutical supply chain and how drug shortages in United States are affected by global disasters. Clear evidence exists that global disasters can have a drastic effect on drug shortages; however, the complexity of the pharmaceutical supply chain itself can also contribute to these problems. The effect of global disasters has an effect no matter the economic status or location of a country. To minimize the possibility of drug shortages, the management of the pharmaceutical supply chain must be better understood, and more effective optimization strategies need to be developed. To streamline processes, predictive analytics can be highly beneficial to the pharmaceutical industry. Demand forecasting and time series analysis are the top algorithms used in pharmaceutical manufacturing that can be used to understand how global disasters effect drug shortages. The information from this literature review will assist in developing a predictive model for understanding how global disasters affect raw material and active ingredient lead times that can result in drug shortages in the United States.

Chapter 3–Methodology

3.1 Introduction

This chapter describes the methodology used in conducting the research needed to develop a predictive model that forecasts raw material and active ingredient lead time delay based on the presence or absence of global disasters and disruptions that have historically been known to contribute to drug shortages in the United States. Understanding the optimal independent and dependent variables that determine what affects raw materials and active ingredient lead times is a crucial step in developing a clear path towards understanding how overall manufacturing production can lead to drug shortages.

To achieve the goal of this praxis, various algorithms and analytical techniques were tested to optimize the predictive model. The chapter begins with a discussion of the process of collecting the raw data. This includes collecting data concerning drug shortages as presented to the FDA by drug manufacturers in the United States and data on the raw materials and active ingredients in those drug shortage products as gathered from the DailyMed database. The chapter then describes how the dataset used in this study was constructed and cleaned to improve its usability in the analysis software. The chapter proceeds to describe the machine learning models tested to determine which would be the optimal choice for this project. Next, this chapter shows how the predictive model is developed, tested, and validated to ensure the development of the best possible model with the greatest possible success rate. A high-level block diagram explaining the methodology, including a brief explanation of each block, is shown Figure 3-1. The sections following further describe each of the methodology steps defined in the block diagram.

Figure 3-1. High Level Block Diagram

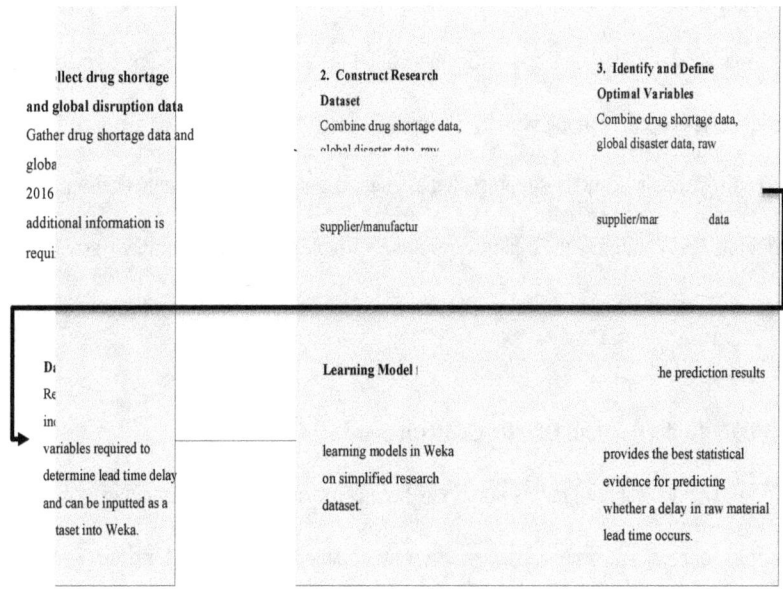

Note: High Level Block Diagram created by author (Zaina Banihani)

A mixture of software applications was used to prepare, visualize, and analyze the data for this research praxis. Such applications used were Microsoft Excel and its various analysis functions like Pivot Tables and Solver, the Minitab Statistical application including the predictive analytics module, and the Weka collection of algorithms. This combination of software applications uses traditional machine learning and deep learning tools to ensure the development of the best predictive model possible.

3.2 Independent Variable Selection

The independent variables for this study were selected based on the previous research conducted on drug shortage factors noted in chapter 2. Each of the potential options for how a drug shortage is caused was broken down into its definition. For example, a medicinal product is made up of inactive ingredients and active pharmaceutical ingredients and is together called the excipients. The name of medicinal product was captured along with the excipients. Similarly, location was given both broad and narrow identifications—represented as state, country, and continent. The same principle was applied to the other overarching variable themes like company size of manufacturer/supplier, rarity, type of excipient, and the global disaster designations.

3.3 Data Collection and Dataset Construction

The dataset used in this praxis has been constructed using data gathered from various sources. The drug shortages data were obtained from the FDA's drug shortage database from 2016 to 2022. For the years 2016–2022, the FDA archive page was accessed using the Wayback Machine, a digital archive for the World Wide Web, to download the drug shortage database for each of those years. As the data presented was obtained in 2022, the drug shortage database was available for use in real time. Based on the compiled list of drug shortages, each product was broken down into its raw materials and active ingredients as gathered from DailyMed, which shows FDA-approved product labeling. DailyMed is a database maintained by the National Library of Medicine (NLM), a National Institute of Health (NIH) institute. For the sake of conciseness, raw materials and active ingredients are labeled as "excipients" for this research.

From the information gathered about the drug shortage products from the FDA and DailyMed, the following was also identified: (a) the manufacturer of the drug product, (b) the city and state of the manufacturing location, (c) the excipient manufacturer, (d) the city and state of the excipient manufacturing location, (e) the type of country the excipient manufacturer is located in (first, second, third, or fourth), (f) the size of the excipient manufacturer by number of employees, revenue, and number of locations, (g) cost of the excipient per kilogram, (h) type of excipient, and (i) the scarcity of excipient.

The historical raw material lead time was obtained from a spreadsheet maintained by the private company of which I am employed, evidence from experts in the pharmaceutical supply chain industry, and excipient suppliers. Like the FDA archive, the Wayback Machine was utilized to verify the raw material lead times for excipients prior to 2022. The occurrence of each excipient was marked, separated by year to see if a trend existed for the lead times, and the percentage difference from the accepted average lead time in the pharmaceutical industry was noted. The delay was calculated by subtracting the individual lead time of each excipient of each year by the expert provided average lead time for the specific excipient (inactive ingredients vs active ingredient). The delay was then split into a categorical variable that is represented by the number of weeks, which were converted to define the extent of the delay as "no delay," "slight delay," and "significant delay." Another way of describing delay is "less than (-1)", "greater than

(1)," or "equal to (0)" the expert provided information. Taking all the variables into consideration, a binary category of yes ("there is a delay") and no ("there is no delay") was derived and determined to be the optimal output variable to determine whether a delay in lead time exists.

The expert judgment average lead time was determined to be 21 days for raw materials (inactive materials) and 28 days for active pharmaceutical ingredients. These values were provided by a professional in the pharmaceutical industry with over 38 years of experience working closely with supply chain management for drug product development and manufacturing. The role expert judgment should play in statistical analysis, however, remains a hotly debated topic. In an article that was written after the October 2017 ASA Symposium on Statistical Inference, industry experts discussed how expert judgment is beneficial and needed for statistical and scientific analyses. Experts and their judgment are considered to be valid due to their knowledge, skill, and experience in their industries and are able to provide content expertise. Expert judgment can be used at any point in scientific research with outcomes that have some subjective elements. This is acceptable because of a theory called subjective probability, which is the probability that an outcome may occur based on an individual's experience (Brownstein et al., 2019). Overall, the use of expert judgment regarding average lead time, which came from an individual with an extensive amount of experience in such matters, allows the data to be acceptable for use in this research praxis.

The global disaster data was obtained from EM-DAT, which is a database constructed and maintained by the Center for Research on the Epidemiology of Disasters

(2023) at the School of Public Health at the Catholic University of Louvain in Brussels, Belgium. The information on global disasters retrieved from their database covers the years 2016–2022. Global disasters were identified for the state and country in which the excipient was manufactured, and an impact assessment and level were determined. The impact level was assigned a variable score from 0 to 4, with 0 being the least impacted and 1 being the most impacted. The level of impact was determined using the Federal Emergency Management Agency's (FEMA) disaster levels scale, which is used to determine the type of disaster that occurs based on severity, size, public welfare, and other factors.

All the data that was gathered for this research praxis was constructed into a single Excel dataset with appropriately labeled rows and columns. Any redundant or incomplete information was removed, which resulted in a thorough and complete dataset. This dataset provided all the necessary information to guide in building and testing a predictive machine learning model.

The variables collected for the each of the excipients in the research praxis are detailed in Table 3-1. The next section discusses how dataset simplification pares down an extensive list of variables to only the most valuable.

Table 3-1: Variables in Research Dataset

Variable	Description	Type of variable
Excipient name	Name of excipient in drug shortage product	Categorical
Year	Year of drug shortage (2016–2022)	Numerical
Drug shortage product name	Name of drug shortage product	Categorical
Type of medication	Medication type of drug shortage product	Categorical
Drug shortage product manufacturer name	Name of the manufacturer of drug shortage product	Categorical
Drug shortage product manufacturer location	Location of manufacturer of drug shortage product (state, country)	Categorical
Excipient manufacturer/supplier name	Name of the manufacturer of excipient	Categorical
Excipient manufacturer/supplier location	Location of manufacturer of excipient (state, country)	Categorical
Excipient manufacturer/supplier location state	Location of manufacturer of excipient (state)	Categorical
Excipient manufacturer/supplier location country	Location of manufacturer of excipient (country)	Categorical
Historical raw material lead time	Historical lead time in days	Numerical
Cost/kg	Cost of excipient per kilogram	Numerical
State vs global disaster	1 or 0 whether a disaster occurred in the state	Categorical
Country vs global disaster	1 or 0 whether a disaster occurred in the country	Categorical
Global disaster subtype - state	Type of global disaster (state)	Categorical
Global disaster impact size state	Impact of global disaster (state)	Categorical
Global disaster subtype - country	Type of global disaster (country)	Categorical
Global disaster impact size – country	Impact of global disaster (country)	Categorical
Type of excipient general	The type of excipient in drug shortage product	Categorical
Rarity of excipient	1 for active ingredient and 0 for inactive material	Categorical
Type of country	First, second, third, or fourth world	Categorical
Excipient manufacturer company size by number of employees	Number of employees in the excipient manufacturer company	Numerical
Excipient manufacturer company size by revenue	Revenue of the excipient manufacturer company	Numerical
Excipient manufacturer company size by number of locations	Number of locations in the excipient manufacturer company	Numerical
Excipient manufacturer company size by number of employees	Size of company by number of employees	Categorical
Excipient manufacturer company size by revenue	Size of company by revenue	Categorical
Excipient manufacturer company size by number of locations	Size of company by number of locations	Categorical
Occurrences each year	Number of times in total an excipient occurred	Numerical
Occurrences in years 2016 – 2022	Occurrence of excipient over each of the years	Numerical
Lead time in each year 2016 - 2022	Lead time of excipients for each year	Numerical
Average lead time	Average number of days for lead time over the 7 years	Numerical
% Difference from Average Lead Time	Percent difference of each year's lead time to average lead time	Numerical
Expert Provided Information	21 days for inactive materials and 28 days for active ingredients	Numerical
Delay	Average lead time – expert provided	Numerical
Delay by how much	1 week, 2 weeks, 3-4 weeks, early, more than 4 weeks, on time	Numerical
% Change from expert info	((Average lead time – 28)/absolute value (28)) *100	Numerical
>, <, = expert info	Average lead time greater than, less than or equal to the expert value	Categorical
Delay – 1/0	1 if the average lead time is greater than expert provided and 0 for less than	Categorical
Extent of delay – slight, significant, none	Slight delay, significant delay, and no delay based on "delay by how much"	Categorical
Yes Delay or No Delay	Yes delay or no delay based on "extent of delay"	Categorical

3.4 Variable Optimization and Dataset Simplification

Once the dataset was compiled, streamlining the variables into usable information for the machine learning software was imperative. To do so, it required taking the categorical variables such as locations (states and countries), names of excipients and suppliers, and global disaster subtypes (both by state and country) and assigning a numerical unvalued variable. For example, each excipient determined to be in a drug shortage product was assigned a number 1 to 652, then the excipient name was found from the list of 1 to 652 and then assigned the exact match number. This process was repeated for every categorical variable to be converted into numerical data.

After the adjustment of categorical variables to numerical variables, it was required to examine the dataset as a whole and determine which variables contribute to the desired output of "Yes Delay/No Delay" and thus cannot be used in the various algorithms. The following variables were determined to contribute to "Yes Delay/No Delay": average lead time, delay by how much, delay, expert provided delay (21 or 28), historical raw material lead time, 2016–2022 lead time, excipients (name), and year. The variables determined to potentially be used as input variables were the following: excipient manufacturer/supplier name, location of excipient manufacturer (state, country together), location of excipient manufacturer state, location of excipient manufacturer country, state versus global disaster, country versus global disaster, global disaster subtype state, global disaster subtype country, type of excipient general, rarity of excipient, and company size by revenue (Small, Medium, Large [SML]). The revenue information was gathered from each individual company's website. The Small Business Administration (SBA) defines a small business to have less than $38.5 million in annual revenue, medium sized business to have between $38.5 million and $1 billion in annual revenue, and a large sized business is classified as having an annual revenue of more than $1 billion. (Novak, 2019)

With the optimal variables identified, the data was pared down further. To do so, the software Minitab was used to run feature selection algorithms on the dataset. The algorithms chosen to run were Cluster Analysis and CART Classification. Cluster Analysis is a type of statistical processing that forms clusters of similar cases and groups those cases together and other cases that are similar together. Minitab shows how the cases are related using dendrograms that explain the similarity between variables. CART Classification creates decision trees for binomial (binary) categorical response that shows if relationships exist between predictors. The results from the in-depth analysis of both algorithms are discussed in Chapter 4.

The variable of "continent" was added and assigned numerical valuation from 1 to 7. The type of excipient was simplified from detailed type to either active ingredient or inactive ingredient and assigned a value of 0 or 1 as well as the rarity of excipient (rare versus common). Ultimately, it was decided that the type and rarity of excipients are idealistically the same where inactive ingredients are common and active ingredients are rare, therefore only the type of excipient was kept as a valuable variable. Company size (SML) was also assigned values of -1, 1, or 0.

Table 3-2 shows the final input variables used to build the machine learning model and an example of the research dataset structure to be uploaded to various machine learning software based on the results from the Cluster Analysis and the CART classification.

Table 3-2. Sample Research Dataset

Country	Continent	Country vs Global Disaster	Global Disaster Country Subtype	Type of Excipient	Company Size	Yes Delay/ No Delay
15	1	1	7	1	1	yes
28	5	1	7	0	0	no
28	5	1	7	0	0	no
28	5	1	7	0	0	no
16	3	1	7	1	1	yes
12	3	1	4	0	-1	no

3.5 Machine Learning Model Development and Testing

For this research praxis, the software Weka was used to analyze the dataset and construct the proposed prediction model. Weka is an open-source software that aids in data preprocessing, executing machine learning algorithms, and displaying visualization tools to assist in developing machine learning models. In the previous section, the significant input variables were identified to predict whether a delay in lead-time will occur. In the following subsections, the potential optimal machine learning algorithms ran in Weka are summarized. The results and discussion of the analysis are detailed in chapter 4 of this research praxis.

3.5.1 Ensemble Learning

Ensemble learning is a type of machine learning algorithm developed to improve the predictive performance by combining prediction options from many machine learning models. As Bonaccorso (2017) explained, ensemble learning is an approach that is best used with weak learners that are trained in parallel or sequentially based on the majority vote or averaging results. Two categories of ensemble learning are bagged/bootstrap trees and boosted trees. Bagged trees have completely built ensembles with training based on random selection of the split and predictions from majority vote. Boosted trees have ensembles built sequentially with a focus on wrongly classified samples (Bonaccorso, 2017). One ensemble learning algorithm was run in Weka using the finalized and simplified dataset: bagging/bootstrapping algorithm as explained in the next section. A visual representation of the ensemble learning is shown Figure 3-2.

Figure 3-2. Visual Representation of Ensemble Learning

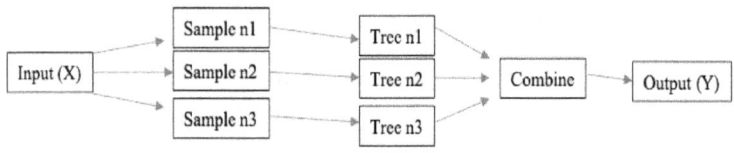

Note: Visual Representation of Ensemble Learning created by author (Zaina Banihani)

3.5.1.1 Bagging—Bootstrap Aggregation

The bagging machine learning algorithm, also known as bootstrap aggregation, is a type of ensemble learning that aids in improving the performance and accuracy of machine learning models and is especially beneficial in minimizing any overfitting issues in a model by taking random groups from the dataset and turning them into classifiers. Using a majority vote for classification methods, the prediction is calculated with the hopes of increasing accuracy. The process is repeated to build decision trees that give the best prediction possible (Gupta, 2023). This type of algorithm is useful for binary outputs as well as multiclass outputs, making it an optimal machine learning technique to increase performance accuracy (Figure 3-3). In Weka, the parameters that can be adjusted within the algorithm are: bag size percent, batch size, calculate out of bag, classifier, debug, do not check capabilities, number decimal places, number execution slots, number iterations, output out of bag complexity statistics, print classifiers, represent copies using weights, seed, and store out of bag predictions.

Figure 3-3. Visual Representation of Bagging/Bootstrap Aggregation Algorithm

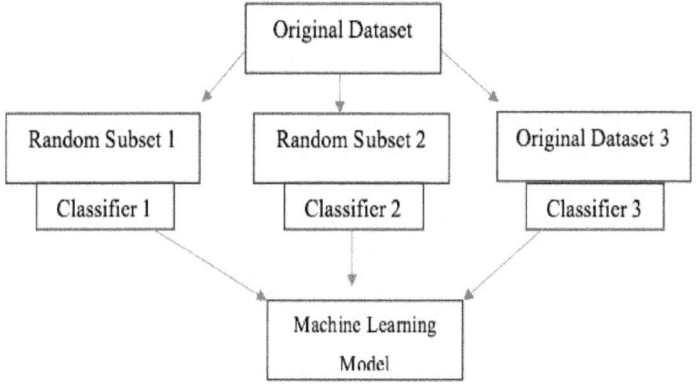

Note: Visual Representation of Bagging/Bootstrap Aggregation Algorithm created by author (Zaina Banihani)

3.5.2 Decision Trees

Decision trees are constructed using a sequential decision procedure. At the root node, a feature is analyzed, and one of the two binary option nodes is chosen for binary outputs. The process is repeated until a final leaf node is reached, which usually represents the desired classification output. The feature separation can change the structure of the tree. Although simplistic in nature, the algorithm functions quite efficiently in its prediction capabilities with most datasets. Figure 3-4 shows a visual representation of binary decision trees (Bonaccorso, 2017).

Figure 3-4. Visual Representation of Binary Decision Trees

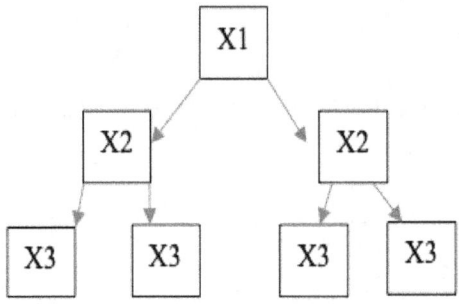

Note: Visual Representation of Binary Decision Trees created by author (Zaina Banihani)

3.5.2.1 J48 Algorithm

The J48 machine learning algorithm, also known as the C4.5 algorithm, is a type of classification algorithm used to build decision trees using information theory. Information theory is the mathematical study of the conditions and parameters that affect the transmission and processing of information (Markowsky, 2017). The algorithm accounts for missing values, prunes decision trees, and aids in determining the rules of the decision trees. The algorithm works by taking the training dataset of samples that are classified and consist of dimensional vectors that describe the attribute value or feature and determining the best split based on the attribute with the most information. The process is repeated at each split using the most valuable and voted for attribute (Khanna,

2021). This algorithm is useful for binary and multiclass outputs. A visual representation of the J48 machine learning algorithm is shown in Figure 3-5. In Weka, the parameters that can be adjusted within the algorithm are: batch size, binary splits, collapse tree, confidence factor, debug, do not check capabilities, do not make split point actual values, minimum number objects, number decimal places, number folds, reduced error pruning, save instance data, seed, subtree raising, unpruned, use LaPlace, and use MDL correction.

Figure 3-5. Visual Representation of J48 Algorithm

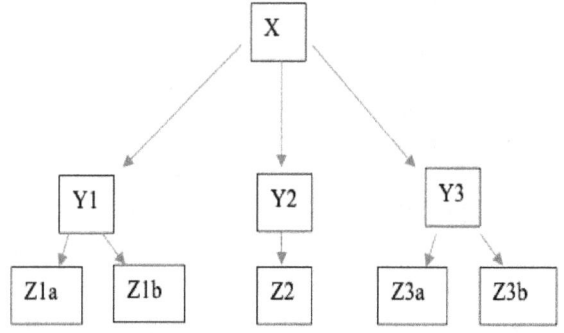

Note: Visual Representation of J48 Algorithm created by author (Zaina Banihani)

3.5.2.2 Reduced Error Pruning (REP) Tree Algorithm

The reduced error pruning (REP) tree machine learning algorithm is a type of decision tree that is a fast learner. The algorithm requires a separate subset of data to be removed from the original dataset to be used for pruning. The REP tree uses a bottom-up approach, which means that each node's subset of data is removed and turned into a leaf with the most abundant option getting assigned to the node. When the algorithm is run again, a node will be removed if the performance of the model is no better or no worse than the run on the training dataset. This process is repeated until the prediction accuracy is at its highest and all redundancies and errors are removed (Elomaa & Kaariainen, 2001). A visual representation of the REP is shown in Figure 3-6. In Weka, the parameters that can be adjusted within the algorithm are: batch size, debug, do not check capabilities, initial count, max depth, minimum numbers, minimum variance proportion, no pruning, number decimal places, number folds, seed, and spread initial count.

Figure 3-6. Visual Representation of REP Tree Algorithm

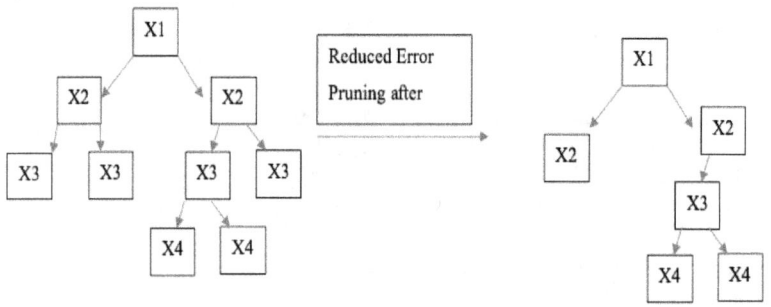

Note: Visual Representation of REP Tree Algorithm created by author (Zaina Banihani)

3.5.3 Supervised Learning of Binary Classifiers

The supervised learning of binary classifiers is an overarching classification of machine learning where the algorithm is trained to make a prediction between two potential outputs. This type of machine learning requires labeled training data that has the input samples and the corresponding output. In general, the output consists of two options like a 0 or 1, true or false, and positive or negative. In the case of this research praxis, the output is "yes delay" and "no delay," which is simplified as "yes" and "no."

Each algorithm run under supervised learning is trained to determine the correct output by learning the patterns, trends, and relationships in the training data provided (Karabiber, 2023). Like other types of machine learning classifications, the performance metrics like accuracy, precision, true positive, and true negative are of importance. These performance metrics will be discussed further in chapter 3, and again in Chapter 4 which presents the results of this research praxis.

3.5.3.1 Voted Perceptron Algorithm

The voted perceptron algorithm is a type of machine learning algorithm categorized under binary supervised learning classification. This is an alternative to the perceptron algorithm, which is the simplest type of neural network. The perceptron algorithm is a single node that takes input variables and predicts labels by calculating the weighted sum of the inputs and a bias called the activation. When activation is greater than 0, the predicted outcome is 1 and when it is less than or equal to 0, the predicted outcome is 0. This standard algorithm is for linear classification and separates classes using a hyperplane and is best used for data that can be linearly separated (Brownlee, 2020b).

In the same way, the voted perceptron algorithm is best for linearly separable data and linear classification but can be used with non-linearly separable data because of its ability to use multiple decision boundaries. The algorithm uses multiple decision boundaries instead of a single boundary. A set of weighted vectors is maintained by the voted perceptron for each decision boundary found, which are associated with a number of votes. The number of votes explain how many times that weighted vector was correctly identified in the training dataset. Although beneficial, the computation is slower for training and prediction, making it less widely used. The equation used in the voted perceptron algorithm is shown in (1) (Smith, 2017). In Weka, the parameters that can be adjusted within the algorithm are: batch size, debug, do not check capabilities, exponent, max K, number decimal places, number iterations, and seed.

$$y = sign(\sum_{e=1}^{E}\sum_{n=1}^{N} sign(w^{(e,n)} * x + b^{(e,n)})) \qquad (1)$$

3.5.4 Classification Algorithms

Classification algorithms in machine learning are a class of supervised learning where the goal is predicting a class on data that is either structured or unstructured. In classification algorithms, class labels are predicted for a dataset that has input data. The goal for classification is to determine what category a new input data belongs to based on the training data that the algorithm learned from. For this research praxis, binary classification is executed where there are only two outcomes for the inputted data (Upadhyay, 2020). A visual overview of how classification algorithm's function is shown in Figure 3-7.

Figure 3-7. Visual Representation of Classification Algorithms

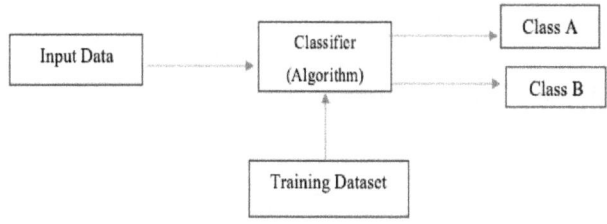

Note: Visual Representation of Classification Algorithm created by author (Zaina Banihani)

3.5.4.1 JRip Algorithm

The JRip machine learning algorithm is a Java-based interpretation of the RIPPER algorithm created by Cohen in 1995 that improves the IREP (incremental reduced error pruning) algorithm created by Furnkranz and Widmer a year earlier (Zach, 2021). The goal of IREP is to produce complicated rules that assist in pre-pruning and post-pruning of decision trees. The goal of RIPPER is determining rules that are identical or increase the performance of decision trees.

RIPPER has a three-step process: grow, prune, optimize. The growth step adds conditions to rules until the subset of the dataset is perfectly classified. At that point the next splitting attribute is identified based on the information gain. As the rules become more specific and are more capable of classifying the subset, previous rules are pruned (or removed) which is the second step. The process is repeated until the rules for the subset are optimized, and the best classification is achieved as well as the optimal decision tree (Sonvane, 2020). A visual representation of the JRip and RIPPER machine learning algorithm are shown in Figure 3-8. In Weka, the parameters that can be adjusted within the algorithm are: batch size, check error rate, debug, do not check capabilities, folds, minimum number, number decimal places, optimizations, seed, and use pruning.

Figure 3-8. Visual Representation of JRip Algorithm

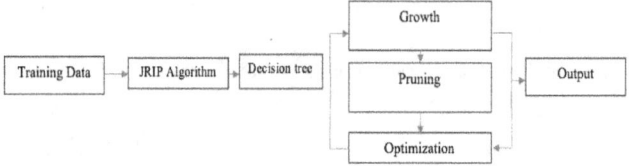

<u>Note</u>: Visual Representation of JRip Algorithm created by author (Zaina Banihani)

3.5.4.2 Filtered Algorithm

The Filtered Classifier machine learning algorithm is a type of classification algorithm in Weka where filters and classifiers are combined and applied to the dataset; the filtering and classification is done automatically. The Filtered Classifier machine learning algorithm is beneficial because it allows for pre-processing the data immediately before applying the filter and classifier. Weka has the base classifier built into the system code, which in this case is a decision tree classifier. When the data is processed using the Filtered Classifier algorithm, the data starts at the base classifier, then is filtered, and applied through the classifier. Any classifier and any filter can be used to process the training data (*Class FilteredClassifier*, 2022). A visual representation of the Filtered Classifier algorithm is shown in Figure 3-9. In Weka, the parameters that can be adjusted within the algorithm are batch size, classifier, debug, do not check capabilities, do not check for modified class attribute, filter, number decimal places, resume, and seed.

Figure 3-9. Visual Representation of Filtered Classifier Algorithm

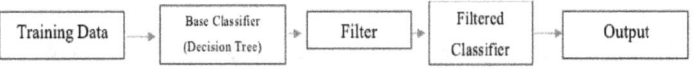

<u>Note</u>: Visual Representation of Filtered Classifier Algorithm created by author (Zaina Banihani)

3.6 Data Preparation for Machine Learning Runs

Before inputting the dataset into the machine learning software, understanding how the model would be validated was imperative. These techniques are helpful in training the machine learning algorithms to be used in building a predictive model. Various validation techniques are available; however, for this research the focus will be on the train/test split method and the k-fold cross validation method. The benefit of validation techniques of splitting data is to see how a model will behave when faced with data or information the model has not seen previously. The following subsections will describe the methods used for splitting the dataset in order to validate the machine learning model developed to make predictions on whether a delay in lead time can be determined.

3.6.1 Train/Test Split

The procedure of train/test split is a popular and simple technique that assists in estimating the performance of a machine learning algorithm, specifically ones for making predictions on data not used in the training dataset. Train/test split is beneficial for computational efficiency with models that could be expensive to train like deep neural network models. The process includes taking a research dataset and dividing it into two sets of various portions. The first set aids in fitting the model using machine learning algorithms and is called the training dataset. The second set acts as a test dataset where the input information is provided, and the model makes predictions on the output and compares it to the expected values. In simplistic terms, the dataset is split into training that the model learns from with known inputs and outputs and test data, on which it executes the learned algorithm to predict the output based on the provided inputs.

The best scenarios to use train/test split is with datasets large enough that allow each dataset (train and test sets) to have suitable representations of the overall dataset. A suitable representation means there are enough pieces of data that show the most common and repeatable information, as well as the more uncommon pieces of information. This type of evaluation procedure is not optimal for small sets of data because of the low quantity of data available to train the model, which prohibits the development of effective learning inputs and outputs. This in turn makes it difficult to effectively test the model and evaluate its performance. The potential for the estimated performance of the model to overfit or underfit is high.

The size of the training and testing data set is one of the more prominent characteristics of the evaluation technique as represented by percentages from 0 to 1. The most common split percentages are 80%/20% (where 80% of the data is training and 20% is test), 70%/30%, 67%/33%, and 50%/50%. No single percentage split is the best for all machine learning problems. The choice is based on what the objectives of the problem are. Different variations of the split percentages were tried in the various machine learning algorithms tested to build the prediction model for this research praxis (Brownlee, 2020a). The algorithms ran for this praxis use the 70%/30% train/test split because of the optimal tradeoff between number of data points for the training and testing data. Figure 3-10 shows a visual representation of the train/test split validation technique.

Figure 3-10. Visual Representation of Train/Test Split

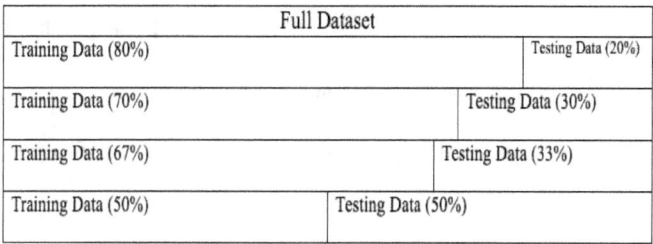

Note: Visual Representation of Train/Test Split created by author (Zaina Banihani)

3.6.2 k-Fold Cross Validation

The procedure of k-fold cross validation is another popular technique that assists in estimating the performance of a machine learning algorithm. The dataset is divided into k equally sized subsets called folds. The prediction model is trained on one of the k-1 folds and uses the remaining folds as a validation set to determine the performance. The process is replicated k times using a different fold as the validation test for each run. Simplistically, many splits are made on the dataset and validation is completed on different combinations of the fold sets and averages the results of each run. This type of validation technique is beneficial because all observations are tested as training and validation and is highly applicable to predictive modeling problems due to its ease of implementation and low bias.

Ideally, different values of k are tested and compared against each other to determine the best model performance among different algorithms. The most common values of k are 5 and 10, as they most commonly provide validation; however, k should be chosen based on the objectives of the problem. Three general concepts can be followed when picking the k value: representative samples, $k = 10$, and $k = n$. Representative samples explain that the k value is chosen in a way that each train/test subset is of a size that is a statistical representation of the dataset. The $k = 10$ idea is that the value is fixed at 10 because through experimentation it results in a low bias and modest variance model. The $k = n$ concept describes that k is a fixed value to n, and n is the size of the data subset that each sample to be held out, which is called leave-one-out cross validation. For this study, various k values were tested to determine the best model performance (Brownlee, 2018). Ultimately, $k = 10$ was determined to be optimal for the algorithms because of the lower chance of overfitting and most efficient assessment of the dataset. Figure 3-11 presents a representation of the k-fold cross validation technique.

Figure 3-11. Visual Representation of k-fold Cross Validation

Test		Train				
Train	Test	Train				
Train		Test	Train			
Test			Train	Test		
Test				Train	Test	
Test					Train	

Note: Visual Representation of k-fold Cross Validation created by author (Zaina Banihani)

3.7 Performance Metrics

Predicting the occurrence of lead time delay is a binary classification problem with the goal of predicting whether there will be a delay or there will not be a delay. With the desired model being classified as a prediction machine learning model, understanding the model's performance based on the data fed back after the run is imperative. The data given after a run evaluates how many predictions were classified correctly and incorrectly.

The performance metrics used most frequently to determine whether a model is functioning optimally and is usable is the accuracy percentage and the confusion matrix, which will be discussed below. In conjunction with these two metrics, the following sections will discuss other performance metrics provided by Weka to determine whether a machine learning model is best for binary classification and prediction.

3.7.1 Accuracy

Accuracy is defined as the ratio of correctly classified samples to the total number of samples in the dataset evaluation. The accuracy value is given as a percentage, where 100% is the absolute best any algorithm can achieve and 0% is the worst (Brownlee, 2016). An algorithm with 100% accuracy predicts all positive and negative samples correctly. An algorithm with 0% accuracy predicts neither positive nor negative samples correctly. Equation (2) represents how accuracy is calculated (Brownlee, 2016). The equation works optimally with generally equal numbers of data samples belonging to each class. In Weka, accuracy is labeled as "Correctly Classified Instances." The accuracy of each machine learning algorithm ran with the research dataset will be presented in the sections to follow.

$$ACC = \frac{\#\ correctly\ classified\ samples}{\#\ all\ samples} = \frac{TP+TN}{TP+FP+TN+FN} \qquad (2)$$

3.7.2 Confusion Matrix

The confusion matrix is a table representation that shows the number of predictions for each class in comparison to the number of instances belonging to each class. Confusion matrices are beneficial in understanding the types of mistakes algorithms make (Brownlee, 2016). The matrix is comprised of four combinations of predicted and actual values, which are true positive, false positive, true negative, and false negative for binary classification problems as shown in Figure 3-12.

Figure 3-12. Confusion Matrix

		Predicted Conditions	
	Total population = P + N	Positive (PP)	Negative (PN)
Actual conditions	Positive (P)	True Positive (TP)	False Negative (FN)
	Negative (N)	False Positive (FP)	True Negative (TN)

Note: Confusion Matrix created by author (Zaina Banihani)

The true positive (*TP*) explains the number of correctly classified positive data points. Simply put, these are the data points that were predicted as yes, and the actual output was yes. The equation for true positive is shown below in (3), where *TP* is true positive, *P* is positive, and *FN* is false negative.

$$TP = \frac{TP}{P} = \frac{TP}{TP + FN} \qquad (3)$$

The false positive (*FP*) explains the number of incorrectly classified positive data points; these are the data points that were predicted as yes, and the actual output was no. The equation for true positive is shown below in (4), where *FP* is false positive, *N* is negative, and *TN* is true negative.

$$FP = \frac{FP}{N} = \frac{FP}{FP + TN} \qquad (4)$$

The true negative (*TN*) explains the number of correctly classified negative data points. These are the data points that were predicted as no, and the actual output was no.

The equation for true negative is shown in (5), where *TN* is true negative, *N* is negative, and *FP* is false positive.

$$TN = \frac{TN}{N} = \frac{TN}{TN + FP} \qquad (5)$$

The false negative (*FN*) explains the number of incorrectly classified negative data points. Simply put, these are the data points that were predicted as yes, and the actual output was yes. The equation for true positive is shown below in (6), where *FN* is false negative, *P* is positive, and *TP* is true positive.

$$FN = \frac{FN}{P} = \frac{FN}{FN+TP} \qquad (6)$$

In the subsequent sections, each of the machine learning algorithms used to build the desired prediction model will be evaluated in the terms of their accuracy and confusion matrix to determine the model's performance.

3.7.3 Weka Statistics

This section discusses various other statistics presented by Weka to determine the performance of a machine learning algorithm. Other detailed accuracy by class statistics provided by Weka is Precision, Recall, F-Measure, MCC (Matthew's correlation coefficient), ROC (receiver operating characteristics) Area, and PRC (precision recall curve), all of which aid in determining the performance of the built machine learning model. The statistics of most importance and that will be discussed further in the results are precision, recall, F-Measure, and MCC. The weighted average is used because it takes into consideration how many objects of the classes are used in the calculation thus giving a better value than a normal average. The *Kappa* statistic, mean absolute error, root mean squared error, relative absolute error, and root relative squared error are presented in the summary statistics however are of less concern.

3.7.3.1 Precision

Precision explains the proportion of samples that are correctly classified. The precision is calculated as a ratio between the correctly classified samples and all samples that have been assigned to a specific class. Precision is bounded to [0, 1] where 0 shows no correct predictions in the specific class and 1 shows that all samples in the specific class are predicted correctly. Equation (7) shows how Precision is calculated where C represents the specific class to be determined, TC is the true correctly classified in class samples, and FC is the falsely classified in class samples. Positive (P) predictive value (PPV) and negative (N) predictive value (NPV) are the replaced factors in the precision equation to determine the correctly classified ratio of either positive or negative classes.

$$Precision = \frac{\text{\# of samples correctly classified}}{\text{\# samples assigned to class}} = \frac{TC}{TC + FC} \qquad (7)$$

3.7.3.2 Recall

Recall describes the rate of correctly classified positive samples and is known as sensitivity or the true positive rate (*TPR*). The recall is calculated as a ratio between the correctly classified positive samples and all samples that have been noted as positive. Recall falls within the bounds of [0, 1], where 0 represents total incorrectness of positive prediction and 1 represents perfect prediction to the positive class. The equation is shown in (8).

$$\text{Recall} = \frac{\text{\# true positive samples}}{\text{\# samples classified postive}} = \frac{TP}{TP+FN} \qquad (8)$$

3.7.3.3 F-Measure

F-measure (F-score) is the mean of precision and recall, which means that it penalizes extreme values of either class and is based on how the classes are defined and the size of each class. If the positive class is larger in size, bias leans towards the positive class, resulting in a high F-score. The reverse occurs if the negative class is the majority, and the F-score is then low. The score is bounded [0, 1] where 0 represents no precision and/or recall and 1 shows maximum precision and recall. The equation to calculate F-score is shown in (9).

$$F1 = 2 * \frac{\text{precision x recall}}{\text{precision+recall}} = \frac{2*TP}{2*TP+FP+FN} \qquad (9)$$

3.7.3.4 Matthews Correlation Coefficient (MCC)

The Matthews correlation coefficient (MCC) is a simplistic form of the Pearson's correlation coefficient. It is a correlation coefficient between the true and predicted classes. If the confusion matrix has good results, then the MCC value is high. MCC is bounded [-1, 1] where 1 is perfect prediction, 0 is random guessing, and -1 is the total disagreement between prediction and observation. The equation for MCC is shown in (10).

$$MCC = \frac{TP * TN - FP * FN}{\sqrt{(TP + FP)(TP + FN)(TN + FP)(TN + FN)}} \qquad (10)$$

3.7.3.5 Kappa Statistic

The Kappa statistic, otherwise known as Cohen's Kappa statistic, measures the agreement between two classifiers who distinguish items into exclusive categories. This statistic looks not only at the classifier's ability but how random chance affects the classification. Cohen's Kappa is bound [0, 1] where 0 shows no agreement between two classifiers and 1 shows perfect agreement. The equation is shown in (11) (Zach, 2021).

$$K = \frac{P_{observed} - P_{chance}}{1 - P_{chance}} \qquad (11)$$

3.8 Validation of Machine Learning Models

Weka uses the historical dataset built for this research praxis to train the various models and learn any characteristics and patterns that may be present in the data. Two of the types of validation methods used in developing this prediction model are train/test split and k-Fold Cross-Validation. The type of validation method used is defined during each machine learning run with the individual algorithm. As stated in Section 3.6.1 (Train/Test Split) and Section 3.6.2 (k-Fold Cross Validation), the split percentage used is 70%/30% and $k = 10$ is chosen as the number of folds for cross validation.

3.9 Comparison of Machine Learning Models

After running the various optimal machine learning algorithms in Weka, the results of the runs were compared. In chapter 4, the performance metrics important for determining the best predictive capabilities of the model are discussed. Of most importance is the accuracy of the model, followed by the breaking down the confusion matrix in order to understand the true positive, true negative, false positive, and false negative prediction. Based on these metrics, the best performing model was chosen as the successful outcome of this research praxis. The results for Hypotheses 1 and 2 were accepted or rejected based on the result of the data analysis as well. Chapter 4 goes further in depth into each of the machine algorithms run for this research praxis and the results associated with them.

3.10 Chi-Squared Testing

In order to conduct testing on if the observed data is as expected, the chi-squared test can be used. The chi-square test is a type of statistical hypothesis testing comparing the observed values in the data and expected values that are calculated to determine if a null hypothesis is true. The chi-square test is best used with two variables, in this case the country and the yes/no delay. The test requires observed data and expected data. The observed data is taken directly from the data set while the expected is calculated based on the grand total along each row and column. The expected values were each calculated by taking the total of each row's response multiplied by the total desired response samples divided by the total number of samples as seen in (12). The difference between the observed values and expected values is the next step followed by squaring that value and dividing it by the expected value. The ending values are then summed to obtain a number to compare against the chi-square table. The degrees of freedom were calculated by multiplying the number of each category -1. An alpha value (threshold for statistical significance) of 0.05 was used to test the obtained sum against. The summed number and chi-square table provided number are compared. If the summed number is greater than the chi-square the null hypothesis is rejected. If the summed number is less than the chi-square the null hypothesis is accepted. The Chi-Squared testing and the associated analysis is shown in Chapter 4 regarding RQ3. (The Chi-Square Test, 2023)

$$X^2 = \Sigma \frac{(O_i - E_i)^2}{E} \tag{12}$$

Chapter 4–Results

4.1 Introduction

This chapter presents the comprehensive results of this study based on the methodology described in the previous chapter. The results of the various machine learning models constructed to predict whether a delay in lead time for raw materials and active ingredients occurs are presented. The validation of each of the hypotheses is thoroughly explained and either accepted or rejected based on the results. Explanation of the data preparation is provided to understand how the optimal variables and validation methods were chosen. The best-fit machine learning model is proposed based on the leading performance metrics as defined in chapter 3, section 3.7.

4.2 Testing and Results–Research Question 1 and Hypothesis 1

RQ1 asks what are the features that impact pharmaceutical raw material lead time delay. H1 states that the features that impact pharmaceutical raw material lead time delay are historical lead time, raw material type, supplier location, and presence of pandemic/disruption/disaster. To validate this hypothesis, two feature selection methods are used to determine the features (input variables) that are significant in determining whether or not a lead time delay occurs. The first method is Cluster Analysis in Minitab and the second method is CART Classification in Minitab. The predictors and significant response variables are described below with the final input variable results discussed.

Table 4-1: Cluster Analysis Results

Amalgamation Steps

Step	Number of clusters	Similarity level	Distance level
1	4	95.3682	0.09264
2	3	74.0297	0.51941
3	2	49.7133	1.00573
4	1	33.3640	1.33272

Note: Cluster Analysis Results table obtained directly from Minitab

Agglomerative clustering of the variables was applied to the data with the 6 narrowed down variables. As discussed in chapter 3, only variables that contribute to the desired output of "Yes Delay/No Delay" were tested. The variables chosen were picked because of their representation of the variables that would be best for defining what a delay is. Other variables contribute to each excipient, but the goal of the praxis is to determine if a delay can be predicted. Based on data simplification, the type of excipient and rarity show identical responses therefore only one of the variables were used in the analysis, "type of excipient". State as a variable itself was removed therefore global disaster subtype in the state is not relevant for further testing and was removed. In the same sense, the DS versus GD state, which represents the occurrence of a global disaster in the state, is removed as well. The goal of the clustering method was to define the groups of variable clusters that show similarity as well as any variables that are distinctly unique to overall determine the optimal variables to use in building the predictive model. Based on the similarity level and the distance level seen in Table 4-1, four was defined as the optimal number of clusters. At four clusters, the similarity level is high (95.368%) and the distance level is low (0.09264). This confirms that the choices made as the final input variables can be considered as optimal. The dendrogram shown in Figure 4-1 explains the variables with potential for being the final input variables to further confirm the cluster analysis.

Figure 4-1: Cluster Analysis-Dendrogram

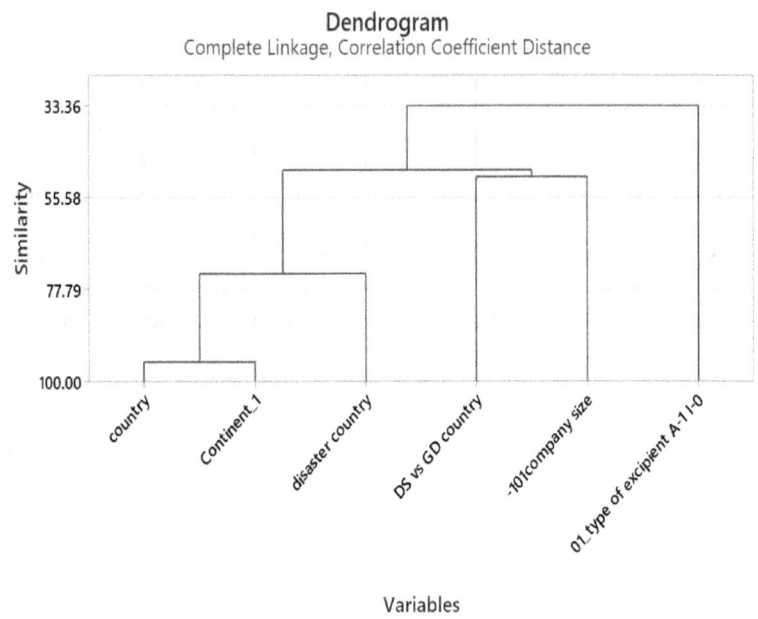

The clade from which type of excipient extends is simplicifolious which can be interpreted as that variable is different than all others in the dendrogram. The country and continent variables are very similar to one another as seen in the dendrogram by a similarity level close to 100% and extending from the same clade and the bifolious nature. The variable disaster country is also simplicifolious extending from one clade however it shows similarity to country and continent. DS vs GD country and company size extend from the same bifolious clade and show similarity around 55%. The information gathered from this dendrogram allows for an understanding of how the variables are similar and can be potential options for the final input variables to be run in the machine learning algorithms.

Figure 4-2: CART Classification

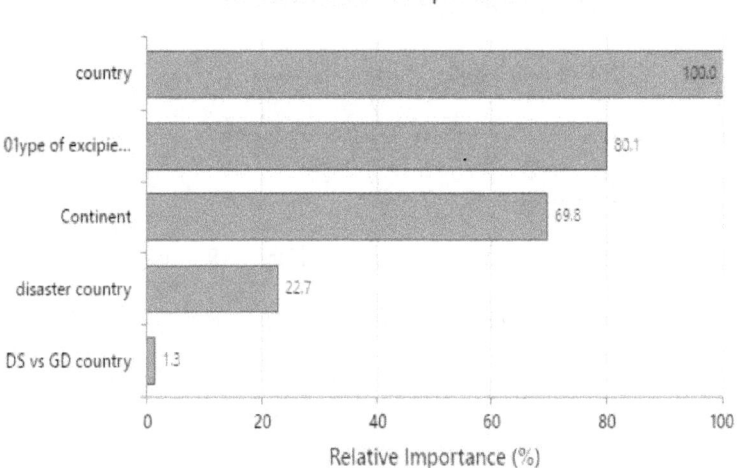

Variable importance measures model improvement when splits are made on a predictor. Relative importance is defined as % improvement with respect to the top predictor.

The same six variables were run through CART Classification to determine the relative importance of the variables to see which of the predictors is most important to the decision tree. Relative variable importance is the percent improvement with respect to the most important predictor and standardizes the importance values for each variable. Variables with the highest improvement scores are set as the most important variable with others being ranked in descending order. Each variable's importance score is divided by the largest importance score of the variables and multiplied by 100% (Minitab Support, 2023).

In the relative variable importance shown in Figure 4-2, the country and type of excipient are both of higher importance where country has a relative importance of 100% and the type of excipient shows 80.1%. The continent showed a relative importance of 69.8% and the disaster subtype for country showed an importance of 22.7%. The occurrence of a global disaster in a country showed a 1.3% relative importance. The company size was not shown on the relative importance however there is a contribution to raw material lead time delay and will be considered as an input variable in the building of the machine learning models.

Based on the results from the cluster analysis and the CART Classification, Hypothesis 1 can be accepted with additional input variables. The results explain that the optimal variables to use as final input variables in the dataset to aid in building a predictive model are country, continent, DS versus GD country (occurrence of global disaster in country), disaster country (the disaster subtype for country), type of excipient, and company size by revenue. These variables indicate that a relationship exists among the variables and their potential ability to predict raw material lead time delay.

4.3 Testing and Results–Research Question 2 and Hypothesis 2

RQ2 asks if a predictive model can be built to forecast raw material lead time delay. H2 states a predictive model that forecasts raw material lead time delay can decrease the chance of production disruptions that lead to drug shortages. To validate this hypothesis, various machine learning algorithms were run with the finalized feature selected data derived from H1 to build the best performing machine learning model. The variables chosen to run with the various machine learning model were chosen due to their direct impact to the desired output of delay. The final input variables are country, continent, occurrence of global disaster in country, disaster subtype for country, type of excipient, and company size by revenue. Each machine learning model built was done so in Weka and the results are presented below. The machine learning algorithms selected to build the best model are JRip Algorithm, Voted Perceptron Algorithm, Filtered Classifier Algorithm, J48 Algorithm REP Tree Algorithm, and Bagging Algorithm, all of which are described in detail in chapter 3. These algorithms were chosen due to their optimal performance with binary outputs which this praxis focuses on and their classification abilities. The performance metrics that were focused on were the combination of accuracy (correctly classified instances) and the TP rate for "Yes Delay." The weighted average of Precision, recall, F-Measure, and MCC were also investigated for their benefit to the machine learning model. The final best performing, and optimized model is presented as well.

4.3.1 Bagging/Bootstrap Aggregation Algorithm

The bagging (bootstrap aggregation) algorithm is a type of supervised ensemble learning used for classification and regression that aids in improving the performance accuracy of machine learning models. The algorithm was run under the Weka default parameters for their Bagging Algorithm to see the model's performance metrics. The results and explanation of the machine learning runs using the bagging algorithm are shown below.

The first run was conducted using the bagging machine learning algorithm with the default parameters set by Weka with 10-fold cross validation. The results shown in Table 4-2 provide the output data from Weka. The accuracy is 77.98% and the TP rate for "yes delay" is 0.553. The precision, recall, F-measure, and MCC are weight averaged to 0.772, 0.780, 0.773 and 0.465 respectively.

The next run was conducted using the same Bagging machine learning algorithm with the default parameters set by Weka; however, this run used the 70/30 train/test split validation option. The results shown in Table 4-3 provide the output data from Weka. The accuracy is 78.36% and the TP rate for "yes delay" is 0.550. There is a slight increase in accuracy and decrease in TP rate from the 10-fold cross validation. The precision, recall, F-measure, and MCC are weight averaged to 0.777, 0.784, 0.775 and 0.484 respectively of which are all slightly higher than the previous run using the same algorithm and 10-fold cross validation. Both runs used bagging with 10 iterations and a base learner. The base learner in this case is the REP Tree classifier.

Table 3-2: Bagging/Bootstrap Aggregation Algorithm–Default Parameters, 10-Fold Cross Validation

Bagging/Bootstrap Aggregation								
10-Fold Cross Validation								
Default Parameters								
Summary				Confusion Matrix				
Correctly Classified Instances		4193	77.9803%					
Incorrectly Classified Instances		1184	22.0197%	a		b	<-- classified as	
Kappa Statistic		0.4598						
Mean Absolute Error		0.3109						
Root Mean Squared Error		0.3938		930		751	a = yes	
Relative Absolute Error		72.3339%						
Root Relative Squared Error		84.9447%		433		3263	b = no	
Total Number of Instances		5377						
Detailed Accuracy by Class								
Class	TP Rate	FP Rate	Precision	Recall	F-Measure	MCC	ROC Area	PRC Area
yes	0.553	0.117	0.682	0.553	0.611	0.465	0.807	0.676
no	0.883	0.447	0.813	0.883	0.846	0.465	0.807	0.889
Weighted Avg	0.780	0.344	0.772	0.780	0.773	0.465	0.807	0.823

Table 4-3: Bagging Algorithm–Default Parameters, 70/30 Train/Test Split

Bagging/Bootstrap Aggregation								
70/30 Train/Test Split								
Default Parameters								
Summary				Confusion Matrix				
Correctly Classified Instances		1264	78.3633%					
Incorrectly Classified Instances		349	21.6367%	a		b	<-- classified as	
Kappa Statistic		0.4754						
Mean Absolute Error		0.3156						
Root Mean Squared Error		0.3979		289		236	a = yes	
Relative Absolute Error		72.9365%						
Root Relative Squared Error		84.8542%		113		975	b = no	
Total Number of Instances		1613						
Detailed Accuracy by Class								
Class	TP Rate	FP Rate	Precision	Recall	F-Measure	MCC	ROC Area	PRC Area
yes	0.550	0.104	0.719	0.550	0.624	0.484	0.814	0.667
no	0.896	0.45	0.805	0.896	0.848	0.484	0.814	0.874
Weighted Avg	0.784	0.337	0.777	0.784	0.775	0.484	0.814	0.807

4.3.2 J48 Algorithm

The J48 algorithm is a type of classification decision tree learning that uses information theory to build decision trees by accounting for missing values, pruning the decision trees during the process, and determining the best rules for the trees. The algorithm was run under the Weka default parameters as a potential option for predicting raw material lead time delay.

Table 4-4: J48 Algorithm–Default Parameters, 10-Fold Cross Validation

J48							
10-Fold Cross Validation							
Default Parameters							
Summary				Confusion Matrix			
Correctly Classified Instances	4189	77.9059%					
Incorrectly Classified Instances	1188	22.0941%		a	b	<-- classified as	
Kappa Statistic	0.4596						
Mean Absolute Error	0.3108						
Root Mean Squared Error	0.3981					a = yes	
Relative Absolute Error	72.3085%			937	744		
Root Relative Squared Error	85.8699%					b = no	
Total Number of Instances	5377			444	3252		
Detailed Accuracy by Class							
Class	TP Rate	FP Rate	Precision	Recall	F-Measure	MCC	ROC Area	PRC Area
yes	0.557	0.12	0.678	0.557	0.612	0.464	0.776	0.648
no	0.880	0.443	0.814	0.880	0.846	0.464	0.776	0.859
Weighted Avg	0.779	0.342	0.772	0.779	0.773	0.464	0.776	0.793

The first run using the J48 machine learning algorithm was conducted using the default parameters set by Weka with 10-fold cross validation. The results shown in Table 4-4 is the output data from Weka. The accuracy is 77.91% and the TP rate for "yes delay" is 0.557. The precision, recall, F-measure, and MCC are weight averaged to 0.772, 0.779, 0.773, 0.464 respectively.

The next run using the J48 algorithm was conducted using the default parameters set by Weka with the 70/30 train/test split. The results shown below in Table 4-5 show the output data provided by Weka where the accuracy is 78.30% and the TP rate is 0.520. The precision, recall, F-measure, and MCC are weight averaged to 0.777, 0.783, 0.772, 0.479 respectively. This run showed a decrease in accuracy percentage and TP rate in comparison to the 10-fold cross validation of the same algorithm but an increase in precision, recall and MCC.

The decision tree developed from the system is shown in Figure 4-3. The tree has 173 leaves and a size of 187. The tree is the same for both validation methods. The direct tree output from Weka is significantly larger therefore Figure 4-3 is a pared down and simplified version of the decision tree.

Figure 4-3: Decision Tree Output from Weka for J48 Algorithm Runs

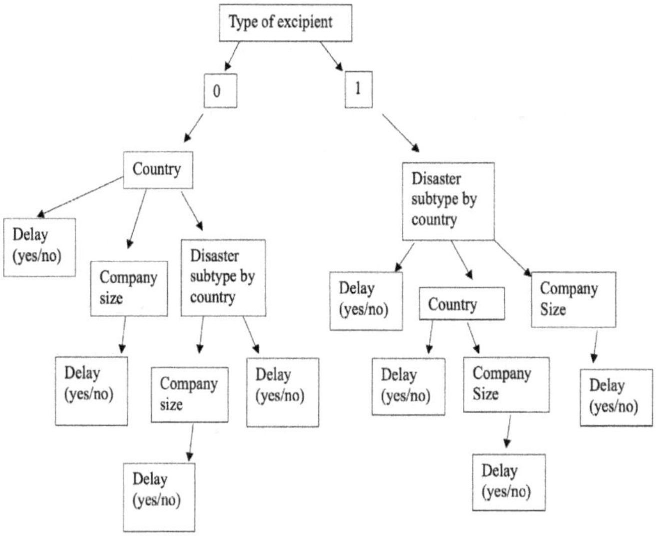

Note: Decision Tree Output from Weka for J48 Algorithm Runs created by author (Zaina Banihani)

Table 4-5. J48 Algorithm–Default Parameters, 70/30 Train/Test Split

J48 70/30 Train/Test Split Default Parameters							
Summary				**Confusion Matrix**			
Correctly Classified Instances		1263	78.3013%				
Incorrectly Classified Instances		350	21.6987%	a	b	<-- classified as	
Kappa Statistic			0.4652				
Mean Absolute Error			0.3087				
Root Mean Squared Error			0.3976			a = yes	
Relative Absolute Error			71.3382%	273	252		
Root Relative Squared Error			84.7943%			b = no	
Total Number of Instances			1613	98	990		
Detailed Accuracy by Class							
Class	TP Rate	FP Rate	Precision	Recall	F-Measure	MCC	ROC Area	PRC Area
yes	0.520	0.090	0.736	0.520	0.609	0.479	0.788	0.648
no	0.910	0.480	0.797	0.910	0.850	0.479	0.788	0.846

4.3.3 REP Tree Algorithm

The REP tree algorithm is a decision tree algorithm that is a fast learner that uses a bottom-up approach to prune the decision tree from the leaves to the nodes. The algorithm was run under the Weka default parameters to see if the model was of optimal performance.

The first run using the REP tree algorithm was done using the default parameters set by Weka with 10-fold cross validation. The output data from Weka is shown below in Table 4-6 where the accuracy is 78.02% and the TP rate for "yes delay" is 0.556. The precision, recall, F-measure, and MCC are weight averaged to 0.773, 0.780, 0.773, 0.466 respectively.

Table 4-6. REP Tree Algorithm–Default Parameters, 10-Fold Cross Validation

REP Tree 10-Fold Cross Validation Default Parameters								
Summary				**Confusion Matrix**				
Correctly Classified Instances			4195	78.0175%				
Incorrectly Classified Instances			1182	21.9825%	a	b	<-- classified as	
Kappa Statistic			0.4613					
Mean Absolute Error			0.3118					
Root Mean Squared Error			0.3980		934	747	a = yes	
Relative Absolute Error			72.5449%				
Root Relative Squared Error			85.8664%		435	3261	b = no	
Total Number of Instances			5377				
Detailed Accuracy by Class								
Class	TP Rate	FP Rate	Precision	Recall	F-Measure	MCC	ROC Area	PRC Area
yes	0.556	0.118	0.682	0.556	0.612	0.466	0.783	0.647
no	0.882	0.444	0.814	0.882	0.847	0.466	0.783	0.867
Weighted Avg	0.780	0.342	0.773	0.780	0.773	0.466	0.783	0.799

The next run using the REP tree machine learning algorithm was conducted using the default parameters set by Weka with the 70/30 train/test split. The output data from Weka is shown in Table 4-7, where the accuracy is 78.36% and the TP rate is 0.550. The accuracy percentage shows an increase, but the TP rate decreased slightly. The precision, recall, F-measure, and MCC are weight averaged to 0.777, 0.784, 0.775, 0.484 respectively which show an increase in comparison to the 10-fold cross validation run.

The decision tree developed from the system is shown in Figure 4-4. The tree has a size of 126. The tree is the same for both validation methods. The direct tree output from Weka is significantly larger therefore Figure 4-4 is a pared down and simplified version of the decision tree.

Figure 4-4: Decision Tree Output from Weka for REPTree Algorithm Runs

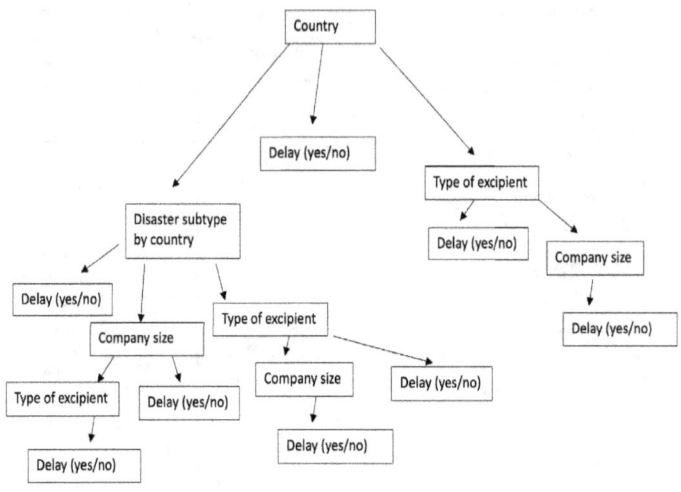

Note: Decision Tree Output from Weka for REPTree Algorithm Runs created by author (Zaina Banihani)

Table 4-7. REP Tree Algorithm–Default Parameters, 70/30 Train/Test Split

REP Tree								
70/30 Train/Test Split								
Default Parameters								
Summary				Confusion Matrix				
Correctly Classified Instances		1264	78.3633%					
Incorrectly Classified Instances		349	21.6367%	a		b		<-- classified as
Kappa Statistic		0.4757						
Mean Absolute Error		0.3207						
Root Mean Squared Error		0.4028						a = yes
Relative Absolute Error		74.1131%		289		236		
Root Relative Squared Error		85.8910%						b = no
Total Number of Instances		1613		113		975		
Detailed Accuracy by Class								
Class	TP Rate	FP Rate	Precision	Recall	F-Measure	MCC	ROC Area	PRC Area
yes	0.550	0.104	0.719	0.550	0.624	0.484	0.773	0.612
no	0.896	0.450	0.805	0.896	0.848	0.484	0.773	0.836
Weighted Avg	0.784	0.337	0.777	0.784	0.775	0.484	0.773	0.763

4.3.4 Voted Perceptron

The voted perceptron algorithm is a type of supervised learning and neural network modeling used for binary classification that uses weighted perceptron to make predictions. A new perceptron is initiated each time a sample is incorrectly classified, and the weights of the vector are reevaluated. The process is repeated until the error rate is minimized. The algorithm was run under the Weka default parameters as an option for the prediction model.

The first run for the Voted Perceptron machine learning algorithm was conducted with default parameters set by Weka and 10-fold cross validation. The accuracy is 74.48% and the TP rate for "yes delay" is 0.387. The output from Weka is shown in Table 4-8. The precision, recall, F-measure, and MCC are weight averaged to 0.731, 0.745, 0.723, 0.352 respectively.

Table 4-8. Voted Perceptron Algorithm–Default Parameters, 10-Fold Cross Validation

Voted Perceptron 10-Fold Cross Validation Default Parameters							
Summary				**Confusion Matrix**			
Correctly Classified Instances		4005	74.4839%				
Incorrectly Classified Instances		1372	25.5161%	a	b	<-- classified as	
Kappa Statistic		0.3315					
Mean Absolute Error		0.2550					
Root Mean Squared Error		0.5047				a = yes	
Relative Absolute Error		59.3191%		650	1031		
Root Relative Squared Error		108.8765%				b = no	
Total Number of Instances		5377		341	3355		
Detailed Accuracy by Class							
Class	TP Rate	FP Rate	Precision	Recall	F-Measure	MCC	ROC Area	PRC Area
yes	0.387	0.092	0.656	0.387	0.487	0.352	0.659	0.457
no	0.908	0.613	0.765	0.908	0.830	0.352	0.661	0.767
Weighted Avg	0.745	0.450	0.731	0.745	0.723	0.352	0.660	0.670

The next run using the Voted Perceptron algorithm was done with default parameters set by Weka and the 70/30 test/train split. The accuracy is 76.81% and the TP rate is 0.564 as shown in Table 4-9. The metrics showed a significant increase in the accuracy percentage and the TP rate in comparison to the 10-fold cross validation run with the Voted Perceptron algorithm. The precision, recall, F-measure, and MCC are weight averaged to 0.761, 0.768, 0.762, 0.453 respectively which are show a significant increase in comparison to the 10-fold cross validation run. Both runs have 1799 perceptrons as explained by Weka.

Table 4-9. Voted Perceptron–Default Parameters, 70/30 Train/Test Split

Voted Perceptron 70/30 Train/Test Split Default Parameters							
Summary				Confusion Matrix			
Correctly Classified Instances	1239	76.8134%					
Incorrectly Classified Instances	374	23.1866%	a	b	<-- classified as		
Kappa Statistic		0.4491					
Mean Absolute Error		0.2319					
Root Mean Squared Error		0.4815			a = yes		
Relative Absolute Error		53.5845%	296	229			
Root Relative Squared Error		102.6895%			b = no		
Total Number of Instances		1613	145	943			
Detailed Accuracy by Class							
Class	TP Rate	FP Rate	Precision	Recall	F-Measure	MCC	ROC Area	PRC Area
yes	0.564	0.133	0.671	0.564	0.613	0.453	0.721	0.537
no	0.867	0.436	0.805	0.867	0.835	0.453	0.727	0.797
Weighted Avg	0.768	0.338	0.761	0.768	0.762	0.453	0.725	0.712

4.3.5 JRip Algorithm

The JRip algorithm, a Java-based version of the RIPPER algorithm, is a type of classification algorithm that implements complicated rules that help in pre-pruning and post-pruning of the decision trees built. The results and explanation for the runs from Weka under default parameters are shown in Tables 4-10 and 4-11.

The first run using the JRip algorithm run was conducted using the default parameters set by Weka with 10-fold cross validation. The accuracy is 76.18% and the TP rate for "yes delay" is 0.579. The output from Weka is also shown in Table 4-10. The precision, recall, F-measure, and MCC are weight averaged to 0.757, 0.762, 0.759, 0.434 respectively.

Table 4-10. JRip Algorithm–Default Parameters, 10-Fold Cross Validation

JRip							
10-Fold Cross Validation							
Default Parameters							
Summary				Confusion Matrix			
Correctly Classified Instances	4096	76.1763%					
Incorrectly Classified Instances	1281	23.8237%		a	b	<-- classified as	
Kappa Statistic	0.4335						
Mean Absolute Error	0.3451						
Root Mean Squared Error	0.4166					a = yes	
Relative Absolute Error	80.2925%			974	707		
Root Relative Squared Error	89.8754%					b = no	
Total Number of Instances	5377			574	3122		
Detailed Accuracy by Class							
Class	TP Rate	FP Rate	Precision	Recall	F-Measure	MCC	ROC Area	PRC Area
yes	0.579	0.155	0.629	0.579	0.603	0.434	0.716	0.553
no	0.845	0.421	0.815	0.845	0.830	0.434	0.716	0.805
Weighted Avg	0.762	0.338	0.757	0.762	0.759	0.434	0.716	0.726

The next run using the JRip algorithm was done with default parameters set by Weka and the 70/30 test/train split. The accuracy is 76.81% and the TP rate is 0.617 as seen in the output from Weka in Table 13. The performance metrics shown describe a higher accuracy percentage and significantly higher TP rate than the 10-fold cross validation of the same algorithm. The precision, recall, F-measure, and MCC are weight averaged to 0.765, 0.768, 0.766, 0.465 respectively which are slighter higher than the run with the same algorithm and the 10-fold cross validation.

The rules developed from the system is shown in Figure 4-5. There were five (5) rules identified which are the same for both validation methods. Each of the rules is shown in 4-5 which is pulled directly from Weka.

Table 4-11. JRip Algorithm–Default Parameters, 70/30 Train/Test Split

JRip 70/30 Train/Test Split Default Parameters							
Summary				**Confusion Matrix**			
Correctly Classified Instances		1239	76.8134%				
Incorrectly Classified Instances		374	23.1866%	a	b	<-- classified as	
Kappa Statistic			0.4645				
Mean Absolute Error			0.3412				
Root Mean Squared Error			0.4148	324	201	a = yes	
Relative Absolute Error			78.8610%				
Root Relative Squared Error			88.4573%	173	915	b = no	
Total Number of Instances			1613				
Detailed Accuracy by Class							
Class	TP Rate	FP Rate	Precision	Recall	F-Measure	MCC	ROC Area	PRC Area
yes	0.617	0.159	0.652	0.617	0.634	0.465	0.731	0.537
no	0.841	0.383	0.820	0.841	0.830	0.465	0.731	0.802
Weighted Avg	0.768	0.310	0.765	0.768	0.766	0.465	0.731	0.715

Figure 4-5: List of Rules from Weka for JRip Algorithm Runs

Number of Rules: 5

Type of excipient = 1 → delay = yes
Company =1 and disaster subtype country = 8 and country = 15 → delay = yes
Continent = 4 → delay = yes
Country = 6 → delay = yes
→ delay = no

Note: List of Rules from Weka for JRip Algorithm Runs created by author (Zaina Banihani)

4.3.6 Filtered Classifier Algorithm

The Filtered Classifier algorithm is a type of classification algorithm that uses the combination of filters and classifiers on the applied dataset. The results and explanation for the runs from Weka under default parameters and adjusted parameters are shown in Tables 4-12 and 4-13.

The first run using the Filtered Classifier algorithm run was conducted using the default parameters set by Weka with 10-fold cross validation. The accuracy is 77.91% and the TP rate for "yes delay" is 0.557. The output data from Weka is also shown below in Table 4-12. The precision, recall, F-measure, and MCC are weight averaged to 0.772, 0.779, 0.779, 0.464 respectively.

Table 4-12. Filtered Classifier Algorithm–Default Algorithm, 10-Fold Cross Validation

Filtered Classifier							
10-Fold Cross Validation							
Default Parameters							
Summary				Confusion Matrix			
Correctly Classified Instances		4189	77.9059%				
Incorrectly Classified Instances		1188	22.0941%	a	b	<-- classified as	
Kappa Statistic		0.4596					
Mean Absolute Error		0.3108					
Root Mean Squared Error		0.3981				a = yes	
Relative Absolute Error		72.3085%		937	744		
Root Relative Squared Error		85.8699%				b = no	
Total Number of Instances		5377		444	3252		
Detailed Accuracy by Class							
Class	TP Rate	FP Rate	Precision	Recall	F-Measure	MCC	ROC Area	PRC Area
yes	0.557	0.120	0.678	0.557	0.612	0.464	0.776	0.648
no	0.880	0.443	0.814	0.880	0.846	0.464	0.776	0.859
Weighted Avg	0.779	0.342	0.772	0.779	0.779	0.464	0.776	0.793

The next run using the Filtered Classifier algorithm run was done with default parameters set by Weka and the 70/30 test/train split. The accuracy is 78.30% and the TP rate is 0.520 as seen in the output from Weka in Table 4-13. The precision, recall, F-measure, and MCC are weight averaged to 0.777, 0.783, 0.772, 0.479 respectively which show an increase in comparison to the 10-fold cross validation run.

The decision tree developed from the system is shown in Figure 4-6. The tree has 173 leaves and a size of 126. The tree is the same for both validation methods. The direct tree output from Weka is significantly larger therefore Figure 4-6 is a pared down and simplified version of the decision tree.

Table 4-13. Filtered Classifier Algorithm–Default Parameters, 70/30 Train/Test Split

Filtered Classifier 70/30 Train/Test Split Default Parameters							
Summary				Confusion Matrix			
Correctly Classified Instances	1263	78.3013%					
Incorrectly Classified Instances	350	21.6987%		a	b	<-- classified as	
Kappa Statistic		0.4652					
Mean Absolute Error		0.3087					
Root Mean Squared Error		0.3976				a = yes	
Relative Absolute Error		71.3382%		273	252		
Root Relative Squared Error		84.7943%				b = no	
Total Number of Instances		1613		98	990		
Detailed Accuracy by Class							
Class	TP Rate	FP Rate	Precision	Recall	F-Measure	MCC	ROC Area	PRC Area
yes	0.520	0.090	0.736	0.520	0.609	0.479	0.788	0.648
no	0.910	0.480	0.797	0.910	0.850	0.479	0.788	0.846
Weighted Avg	0.783	0.353	0.777	0.783	0.772	0.479	0.788	0.782

Figure 4-6: Decision Tree Output from Weka for Filtered Classifier Algorithm Runs

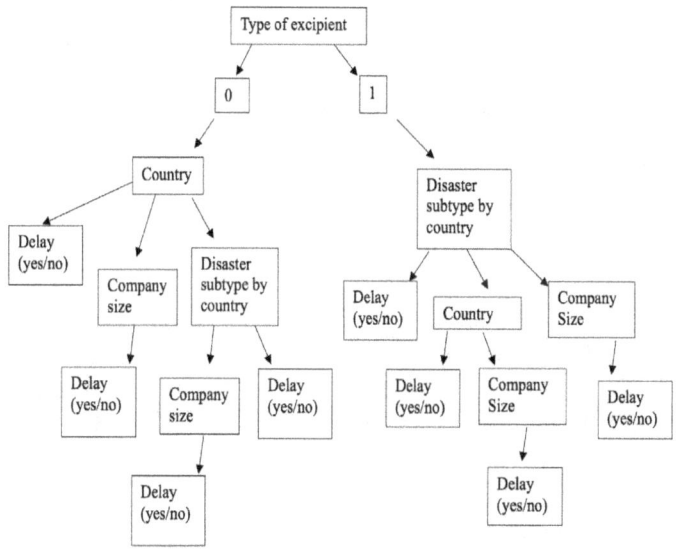

Note: Decision Tree Output from Weka for Filtered Classifier Algorithm Runs created by author (Zaina Banihani)

4.3.7 Default Parameters Versus Adjusted Parameters

The machine learning algorithms runs sown display the models built based on the default parameters provided by Weka. With the base values obtained from the default parameters, adjusted parameters were tried on each algorithm to determine if any further optimization was available. Each of the parameters for the individual algorithm are presented in Chapter 3. Each iteration of adjusted parameters consisted of changing true/false options to their opposite. A seed number that was the default from Weka was changed to a random eight-digit number to see if any changes were observed. The chosen random eight-digit number was the date of which the run was conducted for example if the run were conducted on January 1, 2023, the random seed would be 01012023. Any yes/no parameters were changed to the counterpart. Any value was increased and decreased slightly and significantly to see if any performance metric increase was seen. Each iteration was run individually followed by combinations of the changes and finally the opposite of the default parameters. Unfortunately, each iteration of adjusted parameter machine learning algorithms run showed lower performance metrics. Therefore, the default parameters used are presented and a summary of the extended data is explained in the next section.

4.3.8 Machine Learning Models Results Comparison Summary

The machine learning algorithm runs provided a great number of options to choose from in terms of a predictive model. Tables 4-14 and 4-15 show a comparison of performance metrics between the various algorithms run in Weka using the default parameters. Table 4-16 shows the weighted average for precision, recall, F-measure, and MCC for each of the algorithms run to build the machine learning model.

Table 4-14. Machine Learning Model Results Comparison Part I

Algorithm	Test Mode	Splitting	Accuracy	TPR yes	TPR no	FP rate yes	FP rate no	Precision yes	Precision no	Recall yes	Recall no
Bagging	10-FCV	Default	77.9803	0.553	0.883	0.117	0.447	0.682	0.813	0.553	0.883
Bagging	70/30 TTS	Default	78.3633	0.550	0.896	0.104	0.450	0.719	0.805	0.550	0.896
Filtered Classifier	10-FCV	Default	77.9059	0.557	0.880	0.120	0.443	0.678	0.814	0.557	0.880
Filtered Classifier	70/30 TTS	Default	78.3013	0.520	0.910	0.090	0.480	0.736	0.797	0.520	0.910
J48	10-FCV	Default	77.9059	0.557	0.880	0.120	0.443	0.678	0.814	0.557	0.880
J48	70/30 TTS	Default	78.3013	0.520	0.910	0.090	0.480	0.736	0.797	0.520	0.910
JRip	10-FCV	Default	76.1763	0.579	0.845	0.155	0.421	0.629	0.815	0.579	0.845
JRip	70/30 TTS	Default	76.8134	0.617	0.841	0.159	0.383	0.652	0.820	0.617	0.841
REP Tree	10-FCV	Default	78.0175	0.556	0.882	0.118	0.444	0.682	0.814	0.556	0.882
REP Tree	70/30 TTS	Default	78.3633	0.550	0.896	0.104	0.450	0.719	0.805	0.550	0.896
Voted Perceptron	10-FCV	Default	74.4839	0.387	0.908	0.092	0.613	0.656	0.765	0.387	0.908
Voted Perceptron	70/30 TTS	Default	76.8134	0.564	0.867	0.133	0.436	0.671	0.805	0.564	0.867

Table 4-15. Machine Learning Model Results Comparison Part 2

Algorithm	Test Mode	Splitting	F-Measure yes	F-Measure No	MCC yes	MCC no	ROC Area yes	ROC area no	PRC Area yes	PRC Area no
Bagging	10-FCV	Default	0.611	0.846	0.465	0.465	0.807	0.807	0.676	0.889
Bagging	70/30 TTS	Default	0.624	0.848	0.484	0.484	0.814	0.814	0.667	0.874
Filtered Classifier	10-FCV	Default	0.612	0.846	0.464	0.464	0.776	0.776	0.648	0.859
Filtered Classifier	70/30 TTS	Default	0.609	0.850	0.479	0.479	0.788	0.788	0.648	0.846
J48	10-FCV	Default	0.612	0.846	0.464	0.464	0.776	0.776	0.648	0.859
J48	70/30 TTS	Default	0.609	0.850	0.479	0.479	0.788	0.788	0.648	0.846
JRip	10-FCV	Default	0.603	0.830	0.434	0.434	0.716	0.716	0.553	0.805
JRip	70/30 TTS	Default	0.634	0.830	0.465	0.465	0.731	0.731	0.537	0.802
REP Tree	10-FCV	Default	0.612	0.847	0.466	0.466	0.783	0.783	0.647	0.867
REP Tree	70/30 TTS	Default	0.624	0.848	0.484	0.484	0.773	0.773	0.612	0.836
Voted Perceptron	10-FCV	Default	0.487	0.830	0.352	0.352	0.659	0.661	0.457	0.767
Voted Perceptron	70/30 TTS	Default	0.613	0.835	0.453	0.453	0.721	0.727	0.537	0.797

Table 4-16. Machine Learning Model Results Weight Average Comparison

Algorithms	Weighted Average			
	Precision	Recall	F-Measure	MCC
Bagging 10FCV	0.772	0.782	0.773	0.465
Bagging 70/30 TT	0.777	0.784	0.775	0.484
J48 10FCV	0.772	0.779	0.773	0.464
J48 7030 TT	0.777	0.783	0.772	0.479
REP Tree 10FCV	0.773	0.78	0.773	0.466
REP Tree 7030 TT	0.777	0.784	0.775	0.484
Voted Perceptron 10FCV	0.731	0.745	0.723	0.352
Voted Perceptron 7030TT	0.761	0.768	0.762	0.453
JRip 10FCV	0.757	0.762	0.759	0.434
JRip 7030 TT	0.765	0.768	0.766	0.465
Filtered Classifier 10FCV	0.772	0.779	0.779	0.464
Filtered Classifier 7030 TT	0.777	0.783	0.772	0.479

4.3.9 Final Machine Learning Prediction Model

The final prediction model built is derived from the default parameter 70/30 train/test split of the JRip algorithm. The combination of one of the higher TP rates and highest accuracy makes the algorithm the best performing model to predict raw material lead time delay. The weighted average of precision, recall, F-measure, and MCC show higher mid-range values confirming that the machine learning model is an optimal choice.

The performance metrics for the predictive model are focused on the "yes delay" more than the "no delay" because the instances of "yes delay" are less prominent in the prediction. The predictive model has a TP rate for "yes delay" of 0.617, which means that 61.7% of yes delay instances are correctly classified. The FP for "yes delay" is 0.159, which means that 15.9% of the yes delay instances are wrongly classified as "yes delay." The accuracy is 76.8134%, which is in the higher end percentage rate from the algorithms presented. The weighted average for precision is 0.765 which that 76.5% of the positive classified data in the whole of the positive points (including false positives). The weighted average for recall, also known as the true positive rate, is 0.768 which is 76.8% of the true positives are put into the correct classification (which include the false negatives). The weighted average for F-Measure, which encompasses precision and recall and can be understood as another form of accuracy, is 0.766 or 76.6% which shows the model built qualifies to be a good performing option. The weighted average for MCC, which focuses on each component of the confusion matrix (TP, FN, TN, FP) is 0.465 or 46.5% which means a decent prediction was obtained for each of the categories.

The JRip algorithm is known for its ability to grow a decision tree, prune that tree, and then optimize the tree making it an ideal machine learning algorithm for binary outputs. The algorithm allows for subsets of data to be classified into their appropriate category repeating the process and learning how to decrease entropy ultimately leading to removing of a rule (known as pruning). The process is repeated until the most optimized rules and decision tree are formed. (Zach, 2021)

With the JRip algorithm having the best performing metrics, H2 can be accepted, which is that a predictive model that forecasts raw material lead time delay can be built and can decrease the chance of production disruptions that lead to drug shortages. A model with accuracy between 70% and 80% can be considered a good model, which is what this algorithm and model are categorized (Vallantin, 2020).

4.3.10 Machine Learning Model Run Comparisons

The machine learning models built, and algorithm runs explained in Section 4.3 describe the results for each of the individual runs. Some algorithms performed better than others. This section will discuss any potential reasoning behind why certain algorithms performed better and any similarities or differences seen amongst the models built.

The bagging/bootstrap aggregation algorithm run was beneficial to minimize the chance of overfitting the data. The J48 algorithm is a great option for binary classification outputs because of its ability to determine if any data or values are missing as well as building and pruning decision trees. This can be seen with the accuracy rates being on the higher end of the spectrum in comparison to the other algorithms. The REP tree algorithm works well to achieve a high accuracy while also reducing any errors through pruning the decision tree. The voted perceptron algorithm is a useful option for data that can be linearly separated, and the output consists of binary options however, it did provide the lowest "yes delay" true positive rate which for the case of this praxis is not desirable. The JRip algorithm is well known for its ability to build decision trees based on rules and constantly optimize them to build the most efficient decision tree. The Filtered Classifier Algorithm is useful for its pre-processing skills done on the data prior to applying the filter and classifier.

The decision tree for the Filtered Classifier algorithm and the J48 algorithm are the exact same (which can be seen in Figures 4-7 and 4-10) where the starting decision node is type of excipient and then is split in two by the type of the one excipient type is country and the other is the disaster subtype and it continues until the output of delay is reached. This is interesting because it means that both algorithms put highest emphasis on the same variables.

In contrast, the REP Tree algorithm has a starting decision node of country (as seen in Figure 4-5) followed by either disaster subtype, type of excipient or delay. The disaster subtype and type of excipient go on to further leaf nodes until delay is reached. Different variables had higher emphasis in this algorithm's decision tree than the previous two.

A comparison between the six machine learning algorithms with two different validation techniques showed various agreements and disagreements among the data based on the performance metrics. Table 4-17 shows a comprehensive comparison of each machine learning algorithm and the data associated. The algorithm that showed the lowest accuracy was Voted Perceptron with 10-fold cross validation at 74.4839% which also showed the lowest TP rate of 0.387. The algorithm with the highest accuracy is REP Tree with an accuracy of 78.3633% which had a mid-range TP rate of 0.550. The Filtered Classifier and J48 algorithm run with the 10-fold cross validation showed the exact same performance metrics across the board except for the F-measure. The same concept applies to Filtered Classifier and J48 algorithm runs with the 70/30 Train/Test validation method. Both JRip algorithm runs showed the highest TP rate which were 0.617 for the 70/30 Train/Test validation and 0.579 10-fold cross validation. This confirms that the JRip algorithm is one of the best options for the machine learning model for this praxis. The bagging algorithm, REP Tree algorithm, Filtered Classifier algorithm, and J48 algorithm with the 70/30 Train/Test validation method all showed the same weight averaged precision rate of 0.777 and similar values for each of the weighted averages of recall, F-measure, and MCC.

Table 4-17: Comprehensive Comparison of Machine Learning Models

algorithm	test mode	difference	accuracy	TP rate yes	TP rate no	FP rate yes	FP rate no	Precision WA	Recall WA	F-Measure WA	MCC WA
Bagging	10-fold CV	default	77.9803	0.553	0.883	0.117	0.447	0.772	0.782	0.773	0.465
Bagging	70/30	default	78.3633	0.55	0.896	0.104	0.45	0.777	0.784	0.775	0.484
Filtered Classifier	10-fold CV	default	77.9059	0.557	0.88	0.12	0.443	0.772	0.779	0.779	0.464
Filtered Classifier	70/30	default	78.3013	0.52	0.91	0.09	0.48	0.777	0.783	0.772	0.479
J48	10-fold CV	default	77.9059	0.557	0.88	0.12	0.443	0.772	0.779	0.773	0.464
J48	70/30	default	78.3013	0.52	0.91	0.09	0.48	0.777	0.783	0.772	0.479
JRip	10-fold CV	default	76.1763	0.579	0.845	0.155	0.421	0.757	0.762	0.759	0.434
JRip	70/30	default	76.8134	0.617	0.841	0.159	0.383	0.765	0.768	0.766	0.465
REP Tree	10-fold CV	default	78.0175	0.556	0.882	0.118	0.444	0.773	0.78	0.773	0.466
REP Tree	70/30	default	78.3633	0.55	0.896	0.104	0.45	0.777	0.784	0.775	0.484
Voted Perceptron	10-fold CV	default	74.4839	0.387	0.908	0.092	0.613	0.731	0.745	0.723	0.352
Voted Perceptron	70/30	default	76.8134	0.564	0.867	0.133	0.436	0.761	0.768	0.762	0.453

Although each of the algorithms are different theoretically, for this praxis their performance was well performing for the desired outcome. Any similarities seen assisted in understanding how the data was best fit. The uniqueness of each algorithm and the associated performance metrics showed that the data can also be manipulated in various ways with the hope of bettering the performance metrics.

4.4 Hypothesis 3 Testing and Results

RQ3 asks if all countries were impacted similarly due to disruptions in supplying pharmaceutical raw materials due to pandemics, disruptions, and disasters between 2016 and 2022. H3 states that countries that supply the pharmaceutical industry's raw materials do not show similar disruption rates due to pandemics, disruptions, and disasters. As discussed in H1 validation, the feature selection aided determining the response to H3. The global disasters were originally categorized by state and country; however, to simplify and remove redundant variables, continent was included. Based on that update, a pivot table was created to determine how many countries were included in the research dataset and the occurrence of a delay or not.

A chi-square test was conducted on the countries shown in Figure 4-8 and the outcome of yes delay and no delay. The chi-square test is a statistical test is a type of hypothesis testing comparing the observed values in the data and expected values that are calculated to determine if a null hypothesis is true. The null hypothesis (H0) for this research question is that the country where the excipient is manufactured is independent of yes delay. (The Chi-Square Test, 2023)

As shown in Table 4-18, each country and the corresponding yes delay and no delay data is compiled along with the grand total along each row and column. The total yes delay samples are 1681, the total no delay samples are 3696 totaling to 5377 response samples. Using solely the yes data, the observed values were inputted directly from the table. The expected values follow the calculation mentioned in Chapter 3 and inputted into the table. The table continues by showing the difference between the observed values and expected values, squaring that value, and dividing it by the expected value. Each of the ending values were summed to obtain 440.566. The degrees of freedom were calculated via the method described in Chapter 3 thus giving the value of 33. At 33 degrees of freedom and an alpha value of 0.05, the chi-square table provides 47.400. When compared, 440.566 is greater than 47.400 and therefore the null hypothesis is rejected meaning that the country where the excipient is manufactured is not independent of the yes delay.

Based on this information H3 can be confirmed in that countries that supply the pharmaceutical industry's materials do not show similar disruption rates due to pandemics, disruptions, and disasters. This is valid because as seen during the most recent pandemic (COVID-19), each country was affected but the rate of which they were affected was different. The same concept applies to when only certain countries are affected by natural disasters. In this sense, if one country is affected by a disaster and another is not, the supply capabilities will be different.

To reconfirm this information, data from the World Health Organization was obtained and the countries most affected by COVID-19 were ranked. The top five included the United States, China, India, France, and Germany (World Health Organization, 2021). When compared to the research dataset, the top countries having raw materials that were present in drug shortage product was the United States, India, Italy, France, and China as shown in Figure 4-7. There is a direct overlap between those affected by COVID-19 and the presence of the manufacturer's location leading to drug shortage products. Therefore, reconfirming the difference in each country's capability to supply raw materials.

Table 4-18: Chi-Square Test for Country and Yes/No Delay

Categories	no	yes	Grand Total	observed (o)	expected (e)	(o-e)	(o-e)^2	(o-e)^2/e
Argentina	0	1	1	1	0.313	0.687	0.472	1.511
Australia	2	5	7	5	2.188	2.812	7.905	3.612
Austria	6	2	8	2	2.501	-0.501	0.251	0.100
Brazil	0	1	1	1	0.313	0.687	0.472	1.511
Canada	4	1	5	1	1.563	-0.563	0.317	0.203
China	17	66	83	66	25.948	40.052	1604.154	61.822
Czech Republic	2	13	15	13	4.689	8.311	69.066	14.728
Denmark	2	0	2	0	0.625	-0.625	0.391	0.625
Finland	5	10	15	10	4.689	5.311	28.202	6.014
France	27	72	99	72	30.950	41.050	1685.090	54.445
France	6	5	11	5	3.439	1.561	2.437	0.709
Germany	8	24	32	24	10.004	13.996	195.885	19.581
Greece	2	0	2	0	0.625	-0.625	0.391	0.625
Hungary	1	0	1	0	0.313	-0.313	0.098	0.313
India	1065	613	1678	613	524.590	88.410	7816.408	14.900
Ireland	0	3	3	3	0.938	2.062	4.252	4.534
Israel	31	43	74	43	23.134	19.866	394.640	17.059
Italy	34	74	108	74	33.764	40.236	1618.951	47.949
Japan	2	19	21	19	6.565	12.435	154.625	23.552
Latvia	0	1	1	1	0.313	0.687	0.472	1.511
Netherlands	18	23	41	23	12.818	10.182	103.678	8.089
Poland	3	7	10	7	3.126	3.874	15.006	4.800
South Korea	1	2	3	2	0.938	1.062	1.128	1.203
Spain	15	8	23	8	7.190	0.810	0.655	0.091
Switzerland	5	30	35	30	10.942	19.058	363.208	33.194
Thailand	0	2	2	2	0.625	1.375	1.890	3.023
United Kingdom	1	3	4	3	1.251	1.749	3.061	2.448
United States of America	2437	647	3084	647	964.144	-317.144	100580.519	104.321
Belgium	0	2	2	2	0.625	1.375	1.890	3.023
China	0	1	1	1	0.313	0.687	0.472	1.511
Germany	0	1	1	1	0.313	0.687	0.472	1.511
Poland	1	1	2	1	0.625	0.375	0.140	0.225
South Korea	1	0	1	0	0.313	-0.313	0.098	0.313
Switzerland	0	1	1	1	0.313	0.687	0.472	1.511
Grand Total	3696	1681	5377	**Degrees of freedom**	33	**chi square**	47.4	440.566
Ho - country determining yes delay is independent				alpha	0.05	reject null		
Hi - country determining yes delay Is not independent								

Figure 4-7: Country Occurrences 2016–2022

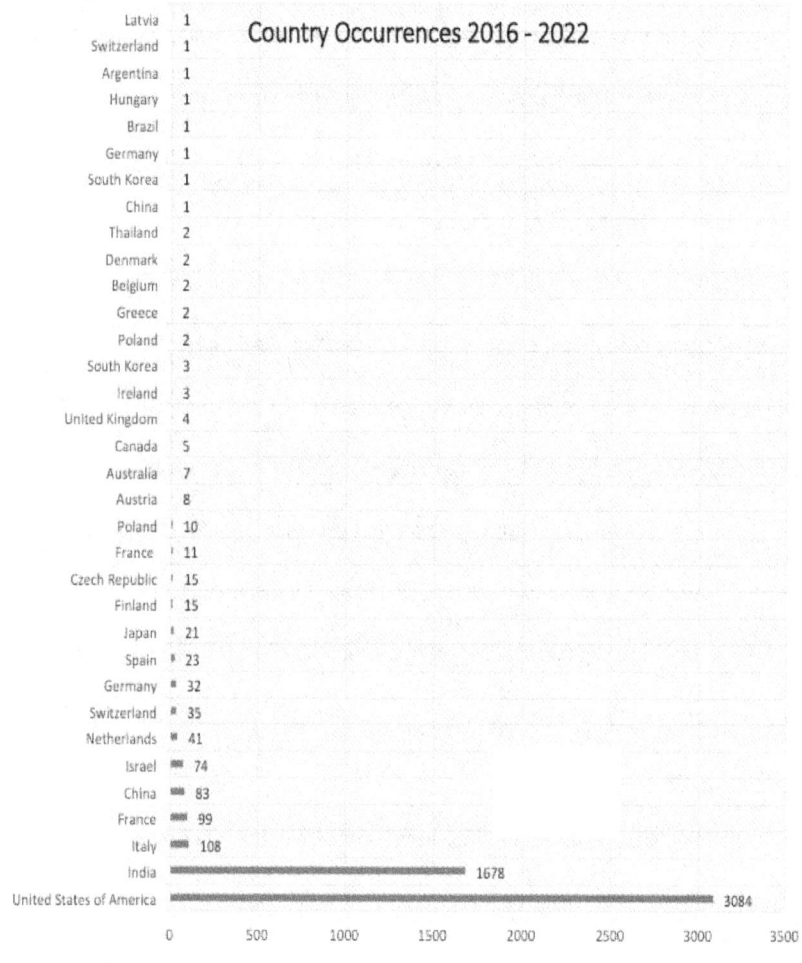

4.5 Summary

The final input variables were determined by running cluster analysis and CART classification. The results showed the best variables to use in the research dataset to run in Weka are country, continent, occurrence of global disaster in country, disaster subtype for country, type of excipient, and company size by revenue. These input variables allowed H1 to be accepted. Various machine learning algorithms were tested in Weka with the research dataset compiled for this praxis. Six of the machine learning algorithms proved that a predictive model could be built to forecast raw material lead time delay that could decrease the chance of production disruptions that lead to drug shortages. With those results, H2 was accepted. A high performing predictive model was built with an accuracy of 76.81% and a true positive rate for the "yes delay" of 0.617. With accuracy between 70–80%, the model is perceived as a good one for the research problem. The weighted average for precision, recall, F-Measure, and MCC are 0.765, 0.768, 0.766, 0.465 which represent a well-rounded and successfully performing machine learning model that predicts delay.

Based on the final dataset, the occurrences of each of the manufacturer country locations was determined, and, when compared to data from the World Health Organization regarding the COVID-19 pandemic's highest cases, four of the five highest nations correlated directly to the research data, thus confirming H3. The next chapter includes a detailed discussion of the results, the contribution to the body of knowledge, and potential future work in the same space as this research praxis.

Chapter 5–Discussion and Conclusions

5.1 Discussion

This research praxis developed a predictive model that forecasts raw material lead time delay based on the most important variables determined through feature selection and machine learning analysis. This predictive model benefits the pharmaceutical supply chain management sector in determining if a disruption in production will occur that in turn may lead to drug shortages in the United States. The data for this research came from the Food and Drug Administration's Drug Shortage Database; EM-DAT (a database constructed and maintained by the Center for Research on the Epidemiology of Disasters (2023) at the School of Public Health at the Catholic University of Louvain in Brussels, Belgium); data provided by a private company; and the use of the Wayback Machine for information from the years 2016–2022.

5.1.1 Discussion – Research Question 1 and Hypothesis 1

RQ1: What are the features that impact pharmaceutical raw material lead time delay?

H1: Features that impact pharmaceutical raw material lead time delay are historical lead time, raw material type, supplier location, and presence of pandemic/disruption/disaster.

The variables determined to be the best final input options were identified using cluster analysis and CART feature selection in Minitab. The cluster analysis showed that the optimal number is four clusters, as the similarity level was high at 95.37%, and the distance level was relatively low at 0.09. The dendrogram constructed provided valuable insight into variables that were similar and those that were distinctly unique. CART classification was conducted on the same set of variables, which showed their relative importance when compared to each other. The optimal variables were determined to be country, continent, DS versus GD country (occurrence of global disaster in country), disaster country (the disaster subtype for country), type of excipient, and company size by revenue. These variables confirm H1 from RQ1.

5.1.2 Discussion – Research Question 2 and Hypothesis 2

RQ2: Can a predictive model be built to forecast raw material lead time delay?

H2: A predictive model that forecasts raw material lead time delay can decrease the chance of production disruptions that lead to drug shortages.

Based on the conclusions from the cluster analysis and the CART classification for optimal feature selection, the final dataset was constructed in a way that best functioned with Weka. Various machine learning model algorithms were run using the final dataset to predict lead time delay for raw materials and active pharmaceutical ingredients. These algorithms were Bagging/Bootstrap Aggregation, Filtered Classifier, J48, JRip, REP Tree, and Voted Perceptron.

A successful and useful predictive model was built using the JRip algorithm, which provided an accuracy of 76.81% and a true positive rate for the "yes delay" of 0.617. The weighted average for precision, recall, F-Measure, and MCC are 0.765, 0.768, 0.766, 0.465 which represent a well-rounded and successfully performing machine learning model that predicts delay. Per industry standards, a model of this level of accuracy can be rated as "good" and therefore is accepted as the best model for the desired output. This achievement provides a significant advancement for risk mitigation strategies in the pharmaceutical industry regarding supply chain management. Based on this outcome, H2 from RQ2 is accepted and confirmed.

Based on the decision trees built for the REP Tree algorithm, J48 algorithm, and the Filtered Classifier algorithm some of the variables showed higher importance than others. The J48 algorithm and the Filtered Classifier algorithm had the exact same decision tree where type of excipient was the starting decision node and based on the type of excipient either country or disaster subtype was the next leaf. The REP tree algorithm has a starting decision node of country which has three leaf decisions to follow which are type of excipient, disaster subtype, and delay. The decision trees both had company size as a leaf further down in the tree.

The variables identified to be of higher importance by the various machine learning algorithm runs are type of excipient, country, and disaster subtype. These are noted as important because of their direct impact on whether a delay will occur with a raw material. The type of excipient directly impacts whether a delay occurs because certain materials are more readily available than others. The active pharmaceutical ingredients are rarer than excipients/raw materials therefore they are less accessible and can impact lead time delay greater. The country is noted as important because the location which a material comes from can have a direct impact on whether a delay is likely to occur. Based on the information gathered from the decision trees and expertise in the industry, third world countries are often more impacted than first world countries when supplying raw materials and experiencing a lead time delay. Country compliments the disaster subtype as the disaster happens in the specific country. The disaster subtype is an important variable because in combination with the country, can lead to the supply and demand issues for raw materials leading to potential delay which coincides with what Ventola notes as an important factor as described in Chapter 2 Section 7. This is direct comparison which makes sense because the disasters have a huge impact on whether a delay will occur. In further research, it would be a good direction to evaluate certain company's manufacturing capabilities in a similar way that Ventola notes (age of equipment, specific manufacturing locations, etc.) to determine if there is a direct impact on lead time delay.

It is interesting to see how much of a difference exists across each of the best performing algorithms that allows to choose which are better for this praxis. With a few exceptions, each of the chosen algorithms could be presented as valid options for predicting raw material lead time delay. As discussed in latter sections of this chapter, it would be fascinating to see how these algorithms would function with multi-class outputs with the same base dataset. It would be a good direction to continue this research in the future.

5.1.3 Discussion – Research Question 3 and Hypothesis 3

RQ3: Were all countries impacted similarity due to disruptions in supplying pharmaceutical raw materials due to pandemics, disruptions, and disasters between 2016-2022?

H3: Countries that supply the pharmaceutical industry's materials do not show similar disruption rates due to pandemics, disruptions, and disasters.

With the knowledge obtained from the final research dataset, RQ3 and the associated hypothesis were investigated to understand the distribution of manufacturing countries that were shut down in comparison to drug shortages in the United States and raw material lead time delay. It was confirmed that the countries that supply raw materials and active ingredients to the pharmaceutical industry do not show similar disruption rates caused by pandemics, disruptions, and disasters. This provides a direct correlation between country and region and the potential to cause delays in production of medicinal products leading to drug shortages. The correlation between the country and whether a delay occurred (yes/no delay) showed the variables are not independent as per the chi-square test.

With a simple idea that evolved into research questions and hypotheses, this research praxis provides an innovative approach to handling pharmaceutical supply chain management. The combination of using federal information and an international database allowed for this praxis to grow into the successful predictive model desired with a promising level of accuracy.

5.2 Conclusions

Quite limited research exists regarding predicting lead time delay in the pharmaceutical industry based on global pandemics, disruptions, and disasters. This is a very complicated topic to study because most of the research focuses on the finished product supply chain or company specific internal supply chain. Virtually all of that research does not cover the supply chain aspect of importing of raw materials and active ingredients from a global perspective, which stands in clear contrast to this research praxis. However, research does exist regarding predictive analytics in the pharmaceutical industry as discussed in chapter 2.

From clustering analysis to prominent feature selection, a predictive model was built using the determined variables. The predictive capabilities of the model were verified and validated using the methods disgusted in chapter 3. With this success, the research objectives explained in the first chapter can be considered accomplished and the thesis statement informing this research in that same chapter can be considered as successfully addressed. From the results gathered during all the testing, it can be concluded that there is a correlation between the existence of global pandemics, disruptions, and disasters and raw material lead time delay, thus verifying the validity of this research praxis.

5.3 Contributions to Body of Knowledge

This praxis set forth new opportunities for determining if a delay in raw material lead times can be predicted with an accuracy of 76.81%. The key contributions to the body of knowledge are summarized below.

1. This research provides several methods that allow machine learning models to be integrated into the pharmaceutical supply chain management sector.

2. The predictive model provides advancement in the understanding of how disruptions that occur globally have an immense impact on medicinal products in the United States that are required by so many people.
3. The research dataset gave insight into which countries globally have the largest impact on the raw materials and active ingredients that are used in medicinal products that have the potential of creating a shortage.

5.4 Recommendations for Future Research

The primary goal of this praxis was to construct a predictive model to forecast raw material lead time delay based on global pandemics, disruptions, and disasters. Although this is a significant accomplishment, a lack of research on this topic nevertheless still exists, which offers a nearly endless opportunity to further expand the body of knowledge on this topic. Summarized below are options to go further in depth that are related to this current research.

The most significant potential for future research is the idea this praxis originally proposed—a forecast model to determine the exact delay in the number of days based on each individual excipient. Being able to quantify the exact number of days that a delay might take can allow for a more organized and structured approach to project management timeline development. As in all industries, the more specific the time estimates can be, the better production can keep up with supply and demand and limit the potential for shortages. With this type of research, time series forecast models could potentially be developed based on the historical raw material lead times, which was a vital piece of information for this research praxis and would be a great opportunity to grow upon.

Another potential research topic, which was once considered for this praxis, would be a multi-class predictive model that narrows down the exact time frame of the raw material lead time delay using the same global disaster information. Rather than focus on a yes or no response as this research praxis does, a multi-class option would provide a more narrow range to be used in production planning. As stated above, the more exact the dates can be, the better the pharmaceutical industry can be in meeting economic needs. In this case, a predictive model would be a real benefit, as seen in this research praxis. Testing various other machine learning model algorithms would be a very beneficial option for future research as well. Lastly, statistically manipulating the quantities of the yes delay and no delay responses to be more balanced and less skewed could be a beneficial option for future research.

www.ingramcontent.com/pod-product-compliance
Lightning Source LLC
LaVergne TN
LVHW012000070526
838202LV00054B/4978